Praise For Ethan

"I couldn't put the book down. I found myself thinking about my own story, and the life events that allowed me to develop into who I am today. His story made me remember to think deeply about the life I choose to live, and to appreciate every I had lived."

—**Sophia Ouloupis,**
Marketing Professional

SECOND EDITION

THE INK OF MY SOUL

AND THE FIRE IN MY BONES

SECOND EDITION

THE INK OF MY SOUL

AND THE FIRE IN MY BONES

ETHAN DEABREU

Halo PUBLISHING INTERNATIONAL

Copyright © 2024 Ethan DeAbreu, All rights reserved.

No part of this publication may be reproduced, stored in a retrieval system or transmitted in any form or by any means, electronic, mechanical, photocopying, recording or otherwise, without prior permission of Halo Publishing International.

The views and opinions expressed in this book are those of the author and do not necessarily reflect the official policy or position of Halo Publishing International. Any content provided by our authors are of their opinion and are not intended to malign any religion, ethnic group, club, organization, company, individual or anyone or anything.

For permission requests, write to the publisher, addressed "Attention: Permissions Coordinator," at the address below.

Halo Publishing International
7550 WIH-10 #800, PMB 2069,
San Antonio, TX 78229

Second Edition, January 2024
ISBN: 978-1-63765-432-3
Library of Congress Control Number: 2023909426

The information contained within this book is strictly for informational purposes. Unless otherwise indicated, all the names, characters, businesses, places, events and incidents in this book are either the product of the author's imagination or used in a fictitious manner. Any resemblance to actual persons, living or dead, or actual events is purely coincidental.

Halo Publishing International is a self-publishing company that publishes adult fiction and non-fiction, children's literature, self-help, spiritual, and faith-based books. We continually strive to help authors reach their publishing goals and provide many different services that help them do so. We do not publish books that are deemed to be politically, religiously, or socially disrespectful, or books that are sexually provocative, including erotica. Halo reserves the right to refuse publication of any manuscript if it is deemed not to be in line with our principles. Do you have a book idea you would like us to consider publishing? Please visit www.halopublishing.com for more information.

I would like to dedicate this book to my mother.
Please know that your sacrifices never went in vain.
We may not have been rich, but you gave Matthew
and I everything we needed.
From the bottom of my heart, thank you.

Contents

Prologue
Quarter Life Crisis — 11

Chapter 1
Sleepwalking — 15

Chapter 2
The Big Questions — 27

Chapter 3
Heartbreak — 40

Chapter 4
The Wolf — 53

Chapter 5
Limit Breaker — 66

Chapter 6
Dreams — 80

Chapter 7
Acts of Rebellion — 93

Chapter 8
Small Acts of Kindness 106

Chapter 9
Forgiveness 119

Chapter 10
Love 138

Chapter 11
Rogue 155

Chapter 12
Utopia 171

Chapter 13
Vision 189

Chapter 14
The Journey 211

Epilogue 223

Special Thanks 233

About the Author 235

Prologue
Quarter Life Crisis

Started April 5th, 2017

"Breathe"

The crisp, smoky air of the night sky floods my lungs. As I lay back, I can feel the vibrations of my echoing heart in my chest. The soft glow of the pale moon is the only thing to accompany me as my mind spills into the mysterious allure of the endless midnight above me. Although the night sky is calm, inside a storm brews, as I undergo a self-inflicted quarter-life crisis.

The rhythmic drumming of my heart grows frantic as thoughts of my self-worth and purpose consume me as I enter the storm. Will my desire for more destroy me? Will the waves embrace me, or drown me? Will the lightning guide my path, or will it strike me down? Does the thunder roar to encourage me, or to make my knees buckle?

The storm may rage and the answers are unclear. Yet, I know I must walk towards it. The stormlight calls my name and I am prepared to face oblivion.

I am about to graduate college with an accounting degree and a job, but I don't remember ever wanting to be an accountant. What child ever dreamed of becoming an accountant? I remember wanting to be a time traveling archaeologist so that I could see the lives behind the old bones that lie still in the museums. I remember wanting to be Rockstar so I could play awesome riffs on my electric guitar and crowd surf in waves of fans. I remember wanting to be a knight so I could protect the weak and fight fire breathing dragons. Yet these days the only bones that feel old are my own. The only waves are ones of anxiety and doubt. The only dragons I see are student loans and credit card companies anxious to give me more debt.

The most exciting decision I have been given in recent times is this: tax or audit?

In high school, I remember being passionate about writing and public speaking, yet somehow this is where I have ended up. I am utterly perplexed...where did that kid go? Am I really *just* going to be an accountant... An accountant?! Am I really destined to be the guy who just ticks and clicks as he mutters financial nonsense while doing your taxes? This is a career path where the only room for creativity is choosing the color of your excel spreadsheet. Why on earth would I want to work for a place where they have people that are proud to have worked 100 consecutive days without a day off? Is that a salary or plain indentured servitude? If someone asked you to give up all your dreams to work on theirs, would you do it? Am I just a sellout?

Absolutely not! My heart yearns to write again! My soul cries when it hears the sound a ballpoint pen makes as it traces across a fresh piece of paper (or in this case, computer keys). Do not confuse the way an accountant hits keys with the way a writer plays them. When an accountant presses a key it's a rough, emotionless, and calculated process. "TICK.... TICK.... TICK TICK....TALLY." On the other hand, a writer greets the keys as old friends; a writer would not play such a brutish melody on such a lovely instrument. With the company of nothing more than a cup of coffee and an idea, they conduct the keys to play in unison in a beautiful orchestra. Accountants make spreadsheets, and writers compose melodies, never forget the difference.

We have all held a dream close to our hearts. Yet, the burdens of the mundane loosens our grasp. This makes me think of being a child. Do you remember when your parents would get you a balloon? You would be so pleased to have it, yet for some reason, you have this strange temptation to let go. The string slides out of your little hand and you are half amused that it simply floats away. However, this feeling fades fast as the regret starts pouring into your heart. You chase after it, making one last desperate jump to grab it, but it is too late. Why did you let go? Helpless, you stand in place and watch the thing you loved so dearly just drift away with the breeze.

When we were children, we did not know any better. However, times have changed. We are no longer that helpless child; we now have more experience with the ways of the world.

My name is Ethan and I am 21 years old, trying to figure it all out. While I certainly do not know everything, I would like to share what I have figured out so far. I believe that through conversation we can tackle the most intimate and intricate challenges we face. It does not matter if that conversation is with a close friend or with a perfectly kind stranger. *I am quite apparently leaning towards the latter of the two.*

The last thing I want to do is talk you to death. A conversation is not much fun when there is only one person contributing to it. I am without a doubt, a young writer. Yet, at the same time, I am an old writer too. I am young enough to believe that I was born for a reason and that words have the power to change the world. I am also old enough to understand that my words alone are not enough to change the world.

I don't really consider that thought to be an arrogant one, but then again, most arrogant people don't think themselves to be arrogant. It is peculiar how our minds work. We often find ourselves suspicious in the face of sincerity. The world has been filled with so many illusions that it is hard to tell what is real and what is fake anymore. Which of these illusions did we put here ourselves? Who created the rest? It is so easy to get lost in the landscape of our own minds. More often than not, it is the simplest of concepts that seem to elude us for the longest periods of time.

I wish to share with you a collection of stories that I have gathered throughout my life that I believe can one day change the world. In order to change the world external to us, we must first control the world within us. I feel that we can come to an understanding together because I am you and you are me. We are all just different versions of the same thing: reflections of each other. Every day we stare into the rippling reflection of our humanity as we try to understand what we are. Although, while that image may seem distorted and unidentifiable, there will come a time when the waters are still. In that moment you will find the answers to your questions.

Chapter 1
SLEEPWALKING

8:20 am

It's a more dreary than normal Monday morning as I stand near the departure board in Penn Station daydreaming about taking the 5:53 pm train home. Better yet, I yearn for a different train altogether . . . one that goes far away. I turn as someone bumps into me and I stare into the crowd. I watch with indifference as the color bleeds out of the world around me and stains the ground at my feet. I am standing at a crime scene and in my heart I ask, *"who murdered creativity?"* I feel a pain from deep within me bubble towards the surface, *"We did. . . no . . . I did."*

When did we stop caring? When did we accept this as normal?

The truth is that we chose to rob the world of color by investing in things and not each other.

We chose this.

We are in a prison without bars, blissfully unaware. Far too often we place our minds in boxes or cages. We walk into our cages and allow ourselves to be domesticated. We refuse to speak out against the norms of society. Instead, we allow ourselves to become too distracted to ponder the abstract.

Who gives a shit about world hunger? Child labor, it's a necessary evil, right? War, it is inevitable? People just don't get along, right? The only thing worse than being ignorant is choosing to be. It is just so convenient for us to turn a blind eye to the ills of society. I mean, we are all just so busy after all. Ripping a country in two from the inside out takes a lot of dedication. We have to debate the extremely complicated concepts of whether education helps people or hurts people, whether women deserve respect, whether love is love in any shape or form, and most importantly, whether "is it racist if . . ." I am so disgusted with what we have come to accept as normal and frustrated that I feel helpless to change it. How can I make a difference when I am only one voice?

What are the magic words that I need to say to make people realize that before the imaginary lines we drew in the sand and the arbitrary labels we assigned ourselves, we were simply *human*?

I dream of changing the world but cannot help to look down at a pair of hands stained red. *How could hands like these create a future worth living?*

The Siren Song of the Cell Phone

Be honest with yourself. In the course of reading this paragraph, you have probably glanced at your phone once or twice. Why is that? The problem is we are addicted to information. This information voraciously deconstructs anything that has ever made us original. We crave the satisfaction of seeing the number "1" highlighted in red on our Facebook feed. We have come to value ourselves on measurements of the superficial: hearts, likes, retweets, shares, pins, reblogs, and views. Upon feeling the vibration of our phones, dopamine floods our thoughts and washes out anything meaningful. I have even experienced people texting me to like their photos. We fervently search for our phones in our pockets and when we pull it out, it turns out there was no notification. We simply imagined it. I often find myself wondering what is real and what is fake. It is becoming harder to distinguish between reality and the glossed over version.

On a subconscious level, we have all battled with the feeling of being inadequate. However, have you ever questioned where that feeling comes from? Have you heard of FOMO marketing? In 1996 the "Fear of Missing Out Phenomena," was recognized by the marketing strategist Dr. Dan Herman. In essence it is condition associated with social anxiety of missing a potentially "better" or more exciting experiences. FOMO marketing, or Fear of Missing Out Marketing, is the marketing strategy specifically designed for the millennial consumer. The focal point of the strategy is to facilitate the fear in young people that they are not good enough. They make you believe that this feeling can only be sedated by buying expensive things? Sincerely, ponder the *audacity* of that statement! Companies are literally capitalizing on your insecurities in order to drive you into being afraid and they aren't even playing coy with the naming of the strategy! The market is tailored to teenagers that are afraid that they aren't spending their time like their idols.

These people are desperate to imitate their glamorous lives just so they can escape their own lives for a few hours. These insecurities did not happen on accident; they were meticulously cultivated by all the brands you love, and frankly, their success is near diabolical.

In order to impersonate adequacy, we mimic what we see on T.V. I remember being 12 and my best friend came to school with a spray tan . . . in February. . . because apparently everyone was doing this because of the reality T.V. show *The Jersey Shore*. The motto of the show was GTL: Gym, Tan, Laundry, because those are all things that matter in life. At the time, I attended a school in New Jersey, the heart of the show. The culture thrived and it was apparent by the number of spray tanned preteens I saw, that I was in the minority. The guys would sport the "crown haircut" and the girls would use the "bump." Although my immediate reaction was to burst into laughter upon seeing all of this, that faded quickly. I was the odd man out in a sea of orange.

Unfortunately, the influences of the show didn't stop at poor taste in style. Everyone wanted to be just as wild and just as "fun" as the cast members. As a result, my friends started throwing parties like them. At 12 years old I had a friend go to the hospital to get his stomach pumped and another that smoked marijuana for the first time. Honestly, these stories are so common that you might even have a similar one.

For me to have enjoyed that show I would have to let my IQ slip a bit. . . off a cliff . . .and into the center of the earth. I just couldn't see what was so great about a show where the main focus was to glorify people that would drink into oblivion. Even though they were all obnoxious, they were nevertheless placed high on a pedestal for all teenagers to see. These were the role models that children aspired to be. We should admire great people rather than the characters on reality T.V. shows. These people are characters; there is nothing real about them.

Although the media may love to complain about the age of millennials and how narcissistic, shallow, and lazy we are, they forget that they are the generation that created this. They forget that they were the ones who created a market of insecure preteens that think that they are losers unless they have the newest Michael Kors bag on their shoulder or Jordan's on their feet. Haven't you realized that what you see in the media is nothing but a giant sales funnel?

If we stripped beneath the layers of the pitch, it boils down to this:

"Good morning! How are you feeling inadequate today?!"

"Low confidence? Put on some Axe Body Spray and all women will find you irresistible!"

"Girls like men with big muscles, but you are so small it is laughable!"

"Be a real man and buy a testosterone booster today!"

"Are you and your friends still playing video games like losers?

"Go buy some beer and have some real fun!"

"That guy you like not paying attention to you?"

"Go buy some new clothes that are little more risqué to get some! Be sure not to act too smart, you might intimidate him!"

We are so much easier to control when we are afraid or distracted. You are too busy looking down at your phone to see the life that is right in front of you. We are too concerned with what athletes, actors, and "musicians" are doing. We are too concerned with their "glamorous lives" to see any value in ours. It feels as if I cannot walk two feet before something is being sold to me. It is as if every inch of blank space is quickly dispatched by the ravenous hunger of consumerism. It is so easy to get pulled into the rat-race; we all want something we don't have. We are constantly lost in the endless spree of "feed" yet we rarely stop to question what we are being fed. They are poisoning the wells just to sell you the cure. Sadly, everyone is lining up, credit cards in hand.

Have you ever heard that saying, *"the things you own, end up owning you?"*

We keep buying things we can't afford to keep up the illusion of being satisfied on our Instagram accounts. We are constantly consuming and devouring every scrap they throw our way. Although the roar of our hunger may be quelled, we are never completely satisfied. That is how the game is played. You will never be satisfied with what you have. There will always be something more, the next new thing. They disillusion you into believing that you are the consumer, but in reality, you are nothing more than cattle being lead to the slaughterhouse. While you impatiently wait for your next meal, you starve yourself of your true identity. This is your true hunger.

As a millennial myself, I am challenging you to see beyond the frivolous use your own creativity to decide what is truly important for yourself. Although our generation gets a bad reputation and is unfairly criticized, the truth is,

- We are the most educated generation in history
- We are open minded and entrepreneurial
- We are socially and politically active

Most importantly, we are ambitious enough to change the world. Let's not be living stereotypes of what others perceive us to be. We are not so standard that one label can define all of us. This goes for any generation. We are all living breathing outliers filled to the brim with youth and passion.

If you take control of your thoughts, you can start feeding your mind at your own accord. Capitalize on the thoughts that set you free rather than buying into the facade that leaves you feeling hollow. Creativity is a precious gift that is unique to oneself. It is not derived from buying a MacBook or drinking Starbucks Coffee. Do not allow yourself to be defined by something external to you. This power is yours and yours alone.

Your mind will never know peace when it is filled with thoughts of inadequacy. In a world filled with people trying to be something they are not, dare to be original.

8:37 am

"Hey Ethan . . .Ethan . . ."

With a tap on my shoulder I awaken from my catatonic fog, and fall into a more familiar one.

My lucidity is slipping away, I can only find the strength to hold it for mere moment of time before I feel my phone buzzing in my pocket. *Why can't I just wake up. . .Why can't I remember?*

I answer Tom, "What's up?"

"It's time to go on the subway, are you okay?"

I laugh to myself because I know the real answer and the one he wants to hear are not the same. In a moment I imagine, *"What if I told him the truth?"*

What would I even say: "No, I'm not okay, Tom. Can't you see that we are standing in the middle of a crime scene? Can't you look these people in the eyes and see that they are crying on the inside?

I'm not okay, I'm not okay! I feel like I'm lost at sea and I am being pulled away by the riptides. Every single day that I work here I somehow manage to sink to a new low. The deeper I sink, the less light reaches me, and the colder it gets. I feel numb and I'm not sure if accepting it is my only choice. I'm not sure if I have enough breath in my lungs to swim back up. Why can't you see that? What happened to your dreams? You're 25 and you are going bald from stress. You actually told me that in order to move up in this world, I have to kiss more ass. What happened to you? What happened to me? Where did I go wrong?!

The truth? How can I tell him the truth when I'm too scared to be honest with myself?!"

Then I dismiss the thought, and with a smile I say, "Yeah, I'm better than ever, let's go."

As I walked towards the turnstile, I found myself smiling because of something he said, "It's time to go." You're right, it is time to go.

Although we walked into the same subway car, we were on two different trains and two different journeys. Sometimes you have to lose something in order to realize how precious it really was to you. Earlier, as I watched the color slowly bleed from my world, I came to realize that it is only a matter of time until I bleed out completely. There will be no tourniquet that will be able to save my life.

As the subway door closed and locked, my mind drifted to a piece of literature that I read in high school, *Death of a Salesman*, by Arthur Miller. The more I worked in public accounting, it seemed like the better I understood Willy Loman. He believed that all you needed to achieve the American Dream was to be well liked, charismatic, and simply want it. He went through his entire career as a Salesman believing that he was well liked and that his moment was coming. He taught his children that school didn't matter, the only thing that mattered was sports and popularity. Time kept passing Willy by and to his surprise, his moment never came. After dedicating the majority of his life to selling, he was fired from his job. This was the beginning of the end. Not only could he not face himself, he couldn't face his family. His dream had died, but he refused to believe that it was his actions that created this reality. Willy was outwardly angry with the world and felt that he was being spited. However, his true thoughts were tamed and poignant, "nothing is planted, nothing is in the ground." He dedicated his whole life to pursuing the American Dream and making his fortune, yet, he lost his job and his legacy.

As I glance at the other wandering souls in the subway, I can see the ghost of that salesman looming over backs that were broken by the weight of their dreams. With a reignited fire in my eyes, I stand with my shoulders back and chest out. For me to bow my head or even grimace is to suggest that this world has given me too much to handle. Luckily for me, I am not Willy Loman; I have the fortune of hindsight.

Although I can empathize with his fear of dying without a legacy; I refuse to sympathize with him. His dreams died because he never fought for them. Willy thought he was born special and destined for greatness. It was that arrogance that was his downfall. He taught me an important lesson: dreams don't come to fruition just by wanting them. To have a dream is a wonderful thing, but too many people spend their time talking about their dream rather than building towards it. A dream is only as powerful as how clearly you can define it. If your dreams are shallow, so will be the grave you inevitably bury them in. When it comes time for you to truly state your goal, do a better job than, "I want to be rich."

8:20 pm

In darkness I depart and to darkness I return. With a deep breath, I shift the gear into park and recline my seat all the way back as I sit in the driveway. There is one prevailing question on my mind, "where has the day gone?" Unfortunately, my fantasy of taking the 5:53 pm train home was shattered due to a certain someone that takes forever to pack up. He never has as much priority to leave as the rest of us since his train ride is only 40 minutes and if he misses his train there is another one every ten minutes. On the other hand, our train ride is an hour and half and if we miss our train we have to wait another 30 minutes. He never really grasped how important it was to us to make that train; he never understood how much of a difference those thirty minutes made. That is typically the case though. Management rarely understands empathy, which makes them miserable leaders. Maybe if he looked into our eyes rather than his Apple Watch he could have seen that. However, his sight was as two dimensional as a text message. To ask for empathy from management is to try and draw blood from stone. Pointless and time consuming.

"Well, this is just life, Ethan, so don't be so dramatic. Some people would kill to be in your position. The job pays you well, so just suck it up. This is what you worked for. This is just what it means to be an adult. You work 9-5 for fifty years and then you retire. Well . . . In my case it is 9-6 . . . And today it was from 6:20 am when I left my house to catch a 7:04 train, until right now . . . as I sit in my driveway. Why can't you just be happy? Graduating college with a job is great success, but I never imagined success to feel so empty."

I'm looking out of the moon roof in my car, searching for the stars in the cloudy black sky.

"Has the fate I feared already set upon me? Has the color truly bled out of my world, leaving me with black skies?"

I close my eyes, and let all fade to black.

8:53 pm

The serenity of silence was abruptly as a voice whispered in the darkness *"Are you giving up?"*

Startled, I opened my eyes, and looked about for the voice that spoke out. I search, but to no avail. I'm alone as I drift aimlessly in the sea of night.

"Great, not only does this job take your time, but your sanity. Get it together man!"

I turn my head to the sky yet again, hoping to see something different. It appeared that something had changed. The light of a single star forced its way through the darkness. A weak smile was chiseled onto my face as I admired its defiance.

"I don't really know much about astronomy, but will you be my north star? Could you share some of your courage with me? Great . . .now you are talking to inanimate objects. You really are going nuts. Maybe it's better to be a little crazy than like everyone else? Maybe I can be like that one star? Maybe I too can stand proud, defiant, . . . and alone? Life is filled with choices, so what is your choice? What are you waiting for?"

I clap my hands together and rub my face, "wake up, it's time to go." I walk into the house and storm the bastille in search of my secret weapon, "Death Wish Coffee", the world's most caffeinated coffee. I cannot help but laugh to myself as I think of the commercial of the Vikings going off to war, "Tonight we dine in the halls of Valhalla!" In order to conquer life, I must embrace the inevitability of death. I can feel its power coursing through my veins. I plant myself at my desk, open my laptop, and start writing. I can either write my obituary or a new story. I will not be consumed by my fears, nor will I consume because of it. No item could ever fill the void I feel looming within me. No, only these hands of mine can craft the piece to make me whole.

Chapter 2
The Big Questions

When I close my eyes it feels like I am falling out of the sky. In the blackness, behind the curtains of my mind, I can see my body cutting through the clouds. As I plummet into the unknown, I feel heavy and light at the same time. I can't tell if I am fading away or losing sight of myself. As I fall, the comfort of time slips out of my grasp and there is nothing to hold onto. Neptune is in retrograde and it feels like I'm being woken up from a daydream. On this fine July afternoon, I find myself facing my mortality. My time is running out and I am afraid that I won't ever return to orbit. As I dream of going forward, gravity pulls me back. How long have I been sleeping my life away? Maybe it is time to wake up and face the harsh reality. I need to embrace that one way or another, be it from old age or an tragic accident, I am going to die.

When considering that I am only 21 at the time I am writing this, perhaps I am being a tad melodramatic. Then again, I have already lived one quarter of my life or perhaps even more than that. Isn't it funny how we all just assume we have one hundred years to live? I mean, how many people do you know that lived to 100? Does longevity run in your family?

Sorry to scare you, but maybe you have less time than you think. I feel that people often overestimate the amount of time they have left and underestimate how quickly they run out of it. Are we born just to die? Or is there something in between that we are supposed to accomplish? Is it all random? Maybe life really is nothing more than a long daydream. Maybe one day we just wake up.

I don't really know why I was born, but I know that I am not ready to die. Life is hauntingly beautiful because it is ephemeral. If it lasted forever, would you appreciate it? All I ever really had was the will to survive, but I never really understood why. Although I may not completely understand what I am here to do yet, I still feel lucky in a way to simply have the chance to be alive, and play this amazing game. As far as I know we are only lucky enough to live this one life, so why aren't you living yours? If we only get one chance, why are we so afraid? We are perpetually procrastinating; we permit pensions to precede purpose. We are so concerned with dying that we forget to live. How bizarre.

Do you even remember your dreams? Are they just a far-off thought? Did they ever mean anything to you? Or was the fantasy good enough? Well, if they ever did mean something to you, I can assure you that you will not achieve them by sitting complacently in your cubicle. You have to break out of the box you keep placing yourself in and let your imagination flow freely. You need to dare to dream once again. As long as you are alive, it is not too late.

There comes a point of time in our lives where we must look inward in order to begin solving life's most ominous questions:

What is my purpose?

Why does this inspire me?

How will I create my legacy?

These are all difficult questions that can only be answered through an honest conversation with ourselves. The first step is to strip your mind of thoughts of the superficial. Wealth, power, and status are not the drivers of your purpose; they are simply distractions. Your purpose in life is far greater than owning a Lamborghini. Purpose is something that originates in our souls and cannot be quantified by material possessions.

So, peer deep into your own soul and see the dream that still lives in your heart.

Think these thoughts when it's 4:57 in the afternoon and you are watching the minutes painstakingly peel off the clock with a masochistic vigilance. The blue luminescent light of your computer monitor can be oddly hypnotizing. Are you just another machine being used to serve a purpose? Desperate to distract yourself for just a few minutes, you allow your mind to wander through the corridor of your thoughts. What are you daydreaming about? Why are the muscles in your face tensing up? Could it be that you are smiling? But why? Why did it feel so strange? Has it really been that long since you thought of that? Ah, what could have been . . . can you feel the longing in your heart for that dream?

Just as you start to entertain the thought of rekindling that once lost dream, you hear an irritating tapping on your desk. You are abruptly interrupted as you withdraw from your fantasy. Your friend asks you "what are you doing?" You look at the clock and it is 5:15 PM. The minutes that you once felt that would never pass are now long since expired. Time certainly has an ironic, and at times, cruel, sense of humor.

When we are young our minds are malleable; we see the world in an unrestricted view that allows us to find our own answers. However, that wonderful window of freedom and exploration is incredibly short lived. One of the most common paradoxes in life is that it is often the people who once told you, "you can become anything and do anything" are the ones who end up trying to force you into being "realistic." What those people don't understand is that your dreams are realistic. It is entirely within your grasp, yet they hammer away at everything that was original about you. Everyone tries their best to hold onto that precious dream of theirs, but each time the hammer strikes, we loosen our grip. Our dreams are smashed into oblivion and we are left standing in the center of a chalk outline questioning how we ended up here. Society may create the mold, but you hold the hammer. Will you chip away at yourself until you are indistinguishable from anyone else? Or will you break the mold?

There is no reset button on life; our first impression is our final one. Although it may seem far off, one day our time will come to an end. While our bodies will perish, our legacy is forever. Do you want to be remembered as the person who always showed up on time for work? Or do you want to be the one that challenged every limitation society imagined for them and won?

I understand that all of this is a lot is easier said than done. Maybe you tried in the past to live your dream and failed. However, it is that very cynicism that is holding you back. When did we all become so bitter, cynical, and pessimistic? The passing of time and our environment has conditioned our minds to think in the negatives. We can almost always see how a situation can go wrong, but rarely spend a drop of energy on imagining "what if it goes right." Just as it can always be worse, can't it also be better?

We go through periods of time when the seeds of the dreams we buried start to sprout again. The fire inside you starts to heat up and you begin boiling with renewed passion to achieve this goal. However, you make a critical error; you start telling people about your dreams. Simply put, sharing your new ideas or dreams with anyone is like lathering yourself in chum and jumping into shark infested waters. Each person lacerates and ravages your dreams with their cynicism and doubt. They make you feel stupid for even having the idea in the first place, let alone thinking that you had a chance at achieving it. More often than not, it is the people we love the most in this world that tear us down, under the false pretense of protecting us. I've been there myself so many times. As a curious mind that has many ideas, it is hard not to share your thoughts. There have been many times where I have been told crushing things by the people I loved the most, even in moments of achievement.

I remember the first time I hit a home run in baseball. I was eight years old and my coach came up to me before I went to bat. He gave me a pep talk because there were two outs already and it was the last inning. He said, "When that ball comes I need you to hit it as hard as you can, just let it fly. I'm counting on you." I walked up to the plate and looked the pitcher dead in the eyes. I was ready for whatever he could throw at me. The pitcher whipped his arm and my target came hurling towards me. I shifted my weight from my hips and my bat connected. I honestly paused as I watched the ball fly off into the distance. I was smiling so hard that my cheeks felt sore, but when I searched for the faces of my parents in the stands, they were nowhere to be found. I felt a small twinge of sadness in my heart, but I ran those bases with pride.

Naturally, when I did see my parents at dinner that night, I was regaling them with the story. My mother was smiling. She was proud and apologized for not seeing it because she was watching my brother play. Although it was a good reason, I was still a little sad. I told my mom, "don't worry, you will see the next one. One day you will even be able to see me on T.V." I had fallen in love with baseball in my youth. I had dreams of being a NY Yankee and playing with Derek Jeter. I even used to have a button-down shirt with Jeter's number on the back that I would wear to school and when I did, I felt invincible.

My father scoffed at me,"The next homerun, huh? I doubt you even it your first one." I was taken aback, and confused. I said, "what do you mean? I hit a homerun, you can ask the coach! The ball flew so far that it hit the side of the school!" He reiterated what he said, and then added, "no way you hit a homerun, and if you did, it was a fluke. You aren't even good at baseball." At this point the tears started welling in my eyes as I balled my hands into fists and clenched my jaw. I asked him, "why are you saying this to me?! I don't understand! I hit the ball! I hit a homerun, maybe if you were there you would believe me!" My mom started to argue with him, "why did you have to say that to him?!" I excused myself from the table and walked towards the bathroom. He called after me and said, "Where do you think you're going?" He started to get up, so I moved faster and locked myself in the bathroom. I suppose my mom stopped him from following me. I sat on the floor of the bathroom and cried. I would bury my sobs in my shirt, doing my best to mask them, because I didn't want them to hear me. When I cried, it wasn't from sadness. Instead, it was from white hot anger. At the time,

I was furious. This was coming from my own father . . .why did he have to say something so cruel?! As a child, I would often wonder if he hated me. These thoughts would fill the emotional container in my chest to the point where it would overflow. When cast into these moments of psychological destruction, I would stew in the intensity of the feeling. That is one thing that has always been very consistent about me. When pushed into a corner, I pushed back. When people doubted me or bet on me to fail, I always looked at it as a challenge to prove them wrong.

In its raw and undeveloped form, my resolve was to prove to my father, and even my mother, that I could do whatever I set my mind to. This story is one of many and it is hard for me to capture the pain of years of destructive words in a few pages. The words thrown at me would grow more destructive as the years went by. In reflection, I understand that regardless of what I achieved, people would always find a way to put me down.

There was at least one silver lining in those moments of despair. This was my mom. That night when my father brought me to tears by tearing down my achievements, my mom was there to pick me back up. At this point I was in my room, laying on my bed with my face buried into my pillow. I could feel the tears flooding on the sheets as I grit my teeth. I kept saying to myself, "He doesn't believe me?! He thinks I'm bad at everything! I'll prove him wrong! I'll hit 100 more home runs, then he will understand! He will see how good I am. . ." My mom walked into the room, and called me by my nickname. Her voice was gentle and prodding, "Bara, come with me." I laid there still, trying to compose myself before getting up. I slowly gathered myself and then followed after my mom. She made me stand in front of a long mirror and then she put my bat in my hands. I didn't understand what we were doing, but then she started speaking, "get into your batting stance."

"Loosen up your shoulders."

"Bend your knees."

"Tighten your grip."

"Swing from your hips."

"Don't listen to what he has to say, I believe you hit it. Keep working hard, practice your form, and you will hit even more."

Later on, she confessed to me that she had no idea what she was talking about. My mother was just repeating the things that she heard the coaches say at practice. Oddly enough, I look fondly upon that memory. Over time, the advice she gave about my batting stance became the foundation of my battle stance. Greatness lies in repetition and as long as I perfect my form, I will be able to execute when the opportunity presents itself.

Life is filled with battles. If the battle does not come from your family, it will come from your friends. Recently, someone who I considered one of my best friends called me a sellout. He said I became a "tool bag," and that I haven't made time for him because I am always doing my own thing. He tried to qualify his feelings to me by saying, "I'm not the only one who feels this way so you know." I just never really expected that from him. This hurt me, more than he will ever realize. It's a real shame when someone you have been there for when the cards were down and they were ready to fold turns their back on you. It's now my turn to worry about the hand I have been dealt and I have to be careful how I play it.

I know that his feelings came from a place of insecurity. He felt that I was leaving him behind by moving forward. It's sad when you lose people while in the pursuit of your dreams, but, I suppose that's why they say, "it's lonely at the top." Before you go pursuing your dreams, be sure that you are ready to take the risk of being misunderstood and losing friends. This comes with the territory. You just have to decide what is more important to you. Are your dreams more important than a mediocre friendship? Maybe it was the people that you have been surrounding yourself with all this time that have been holding you back? Although that friendship may or may not have ended, I am still grateful for the memories. I'll always carry the good times in my heart and bear the scars of the bad on my soul. In a way, I appreciate everyone who ever doubted me and told me I was bound for failure. Every time they put me down, they poured gasoline on a soul that was already on fire. They couldn't drown my spirit with all the negativity in the world.

While walking the path of a loner, I taught myself, "as long as I can respect myself at the end of the day, nothing else matters." I decided that, "I will always fight for what I believe in, even if I have to fight alone. I will not let them beat me into submission. I will not go down."

There will always be people who want to put you down, but as long as you have at least one person who believes in you, that is all that matters. Sometimes, the only person that believes in you, is you, but that is okay. As long as you understand your own mission, nothing else matters. I want you to be bold enough to ask more from yourself every single day. I want you to have the audacity to say, "I don't care about your opinion, because I know mine." I know I can accomplish my dreams.

We all have questions that burn inside of us that demand answering. You have to go to that place where you buried your dreams. You can either go there with flowers or a shovel. The most important questions you have to ask yourself is, "Was it just an idea? Or was it my calling? Why does it come to my mind whenever I day dream? Is *this* . . .all there really is to life?"

One early morning, as I was driving to college, a thought occurred to me,

"If you aren't living you are just dying."

We are all alive, but how we spend that time determines if we are living. The only guarantee in life that we have is that death awaits. I don't know much about the afterlife, but I do know about legacy. I understand that if I live a life worth remembering, I will never be forgotten. I have slowly come to realize that my dream isn't a singular thing, it's far more abstract. My dream is to change the world. I want to reach the hearts of all people and remind them what it is to dream and to have hope. When I look around I see many tired eyes; people that have been beaten down by the humdrum of the world. Sometimes I want to run up to them, and shake them, "we are alive! So, start living!"

The problem is that I am afraid. I am afraid of dying a hypocrite. When I look in the mirror, my eyes can be just as tired as the ones I want to inspire. I can see the wrinkles on my forehead from two decades of thoughts. My eyes have black bags under them. I can see how much I have aged and when I blur my eyes, I can see myself in another 40 years if this life continues. When I look at that man, it shakes me to the core. I can only see him for a second as my eyes adjust to the lights. However, he is there watching me, just as I am watching him. It's like he is staring into my soul as his eyes are filled with a regret. I can see him yelling, but I can't hear what he's saying. He looks so desperate, like he is pleading with me.

I want people to believe in their dreams, but I don't know if I am strong enough to make mine a reality. I don't have the answers that you are looking for; hell, I don't even have all the answers to mine. However, I do have stories. I have learned that despite what all these "gurus" are selling you, there is no secret recipe for success. There is no cookie cutter model to guarantee you a six-figure job for the next 50 years.

Shakespeare said, "all the world's a stage" but I'm tired of the act. I'm tired of pretending that I am satisfied. I think it's time to draw the curtains on the stage and start writing in the pages of my book. I have a few options in this book of mine:

I can be the nefarious villain. I can be the perfect antagonist, the one that is ready to watch the world burn as he smokes his cigar and drinks his whiskey neat. I could be bitter and cruel; I could preach an ideology that those who believe in dreams are nothing but fools, too naive to accept the reality of this world. I could live off the satisfaction of destroying the dreams of others because I never reached mine.

I could be a bystander or a spectator in this story. It is easy to go through the motions; if I put my head down and work to build my career, perhaps I can be happy. Maybe happiness in life is as simple as getting a job, buying a house, and raising a family. I could work 9-6 on the weekdays, and on the weekends, I can mow the lawn. Maybe take my wife and kids to the local diner and share some laughs.

I could be nothing more than plot fodder. I could exist for no other purpose but to progress the story in a small, but not so meaningful way. Maybe it is easier to just go through life without any grand dreams so that I don't have to cope with the pressure that comes with them. Life is probably easier if I don't cause any ripples. Would I rather just watch others achieve their dreams? Is it just that I am not that kind of person? While it just wasn't my fate to be lucky enough to live a life like them, I can still live vicariously through them.

If any of those options interest you or sound appealing, that's okay. There is no shame in being happy with your job and wanting to climb the corporate ladder. My story isn't yours; you get to choose the hero. Who I could be and who I want to be are two different things. Although I could be the villain, I would rather be the hero to my own story. I would rather live in pursuit of a dream than never mustering the courage to have one.

Regardless of the outcome, I was given the chance to fill these pages. So, here I go. There are no scripts, no teleprompter, and there is no voice in my ear telling me what to say. This story has just begun and it started with me understanding what the old man in the mirror was trying to say to me. Although his words couldn't reach me, I heard what was in his heart, "Don't be afraid to live. I was. . . but you still have a chance to change! Don't become me, FIGHT!"

Every morning when my alarm sounds, I remember that old man. When I go to the bathroom and turn the lights on, I expect to see him looking back at me. However, he's gone. He already told me what he needed to and now is the time to start building towards my goal. My immediate thought is if I'm lucky, I'll never see that old man again. Then I realized that for me to think that way means I entirely missed the point.

Chapter 3
Heartbreak

I still remember the night she told us. I was seven years old at the time and I remember sitting at the edge of the stairs. I stared in horror as I heard my father yell at my mother. She was sobbing, begging, and pleading with him to stay. My little brother, Matthew, came towards the stairs so he could listen too, but I shooed him away. Although I was young, something inside me said, "you are the older brother, you need to protect him." The only problem was, I didn't know how to protect him. All I could do was try to preserve his innocence by shielding his heart with my own.

The shrapnel flew indiscriminately and ripped into the four walls of my home. I did my best to protect him, but I knew that no matter how hard I may have tried, I couldn't save him from it all.

I could hear my mother make her way to the stairs, her sobs echoing in her cupped hand. I snapped out of my catatonic state and scrambled to get to my room as quickly and as quietly as possible. I was also trying to shield my mom from the knowledge that I had heard all that had just transpired. I grasped my chest and winced with pain. With each step, I could feel the still hot shrapnel cutting my heart to ribbons.

My mother called my brother and I out of our room. She brought us into the bathroom and crouched down to look us in our eyes. My jaw was tight and my teeth clamped down hard, but I didn't know why. I kept trying to reassure myself in my mind that everything was going to be okay, but I knew that it was a lie. She was just saying words, but I was losing my senses. All I could hear was the pace of my heart as it pounded harder and harder in my chest. Everything froze when I heard, "Your Dad and I are going to get a divorce, it means that we won't be living together anymore. We both still love you very much and it's not *your*. . ." My heart stopped and for the first time in my life hot tears rolled down my face from a pain that I could not see. This was terrifying to me.

I understand that many children in my generation grew up with divorced parents. Although divorce has become unfortunately common in the United States, with as many as 50% of marriages ending in divorce, this experience was the harbinger of a period of dramatic change in my life. It is part of my identity.

My parents began their divorce when I was about seven years old, two weeks after I made my Holy Communion. My father had been unfaithful to my mother and she confronted him about it. Little did he know that he broke more than one heart that day.

It is tempting to get into the story of my mother and father, but that is not my story to tell. This is my third attempt at writing about this part of my life and it feels like the words are fighting me with each keystroke. I have no right to speak on my mother's or my father's behalf and I will respect that.

The story I tell is mine, and mine alone...

Although the reality I was familiar with was shattered, life went on, I still had school on Monday. At the time, I was going to Catholic elementary school and I had confided in some of my friends about what was happening. I tried to communicate my confusion and pain to them, but they just couldn't understand. Word got around about what was happening between my parents and the bullies caught a whiff of my weakness. You see, I had been very well acquainted with these three jerks since I started school. They used to pick on a few other kids and I would always stand up for them. They hated me for ruining their fun. Now that they could physically see that I was weak and in pain. They jumped at the opportunity. They would tell me how it was my fault that my parents were divorcing. They would call me a sinner and tell me how much my parents hated me and couldn't wait to leave. They stated that this was God was punishing me for being such an awful person and that I was getting what I deserved.

I know that none of these things they said to me were true now, but back then, things were different. *You know when you hear something enough, you start to believe it?* I really came to believe that I was worthless and in some messed up way, everything that was happening was because I wasn't good enough.

The broken glass in my chest tore into me more and more with each passing day, yet, I never grimaced, winced, or shed a single tear in front of those kids or anyone for that matter. Every day after school, for about three weeks, I would go to my backyard. Once there I would climb the ladder of my playset, bury my head in my knees, and cry. I would run to the backyard because I could feel the tears fighting their way out. However, one day they just wouldn't come. The hot tears that once sprinted down my cheeks and into the splinters of wood beneath me froze over the shattered pieces of my heart. In doing so, they captured all the pain inside. I felt numb, but at least I didn't feel the pain.

On that day I made a choice to leave that part of me behind and to lock all the pain inside. Although I had believed that I was sinner, I remembered another important dialogue when I was up there. The dialogue of "you are the big brother, and you need to set an example." I don't really know why it came to me when it did, but it did. That thought was the last good thought I had in me and I clung onto it. I would be strong for my brother, for Matthew, and I would show him a path away from the pain as I carved it out.

By no means did I even come close to being the perfect brother to Matthew, but I tried. In the years to come, my role was more of a parental role than that of a sibling. I would check his homework every night. I would try to teach him new things or even get him to just play catch with me like father and son would do in the movies. I just wanted to protect him from the pain that I felt in my heart. I would try to carry it all for him. However, my one regret was that I struggled to show him love. My heart was filled to the brim trying to hold the pain for both of us that I just didn't have the space to feel love. It was so hard for me show love to anyone anymore. That feeling just would not come naturally to me. When I numbed my heart, it wasn't just to the pain, it was to everything. My heart stayed that way for a long time.

When I returned to school the next day, anger and intensity seethed out of me. I could feel the red smoke swirl around me as my rage boiled towards the surface. One of the jerks came up to me and said, "how's it going "He-Ethan?" This was a reference to the word "heathen." Kids are just *so creative*. He continued to prod, "Got nothing to say? Huh? I know your dad left, but I didn't realize he took your words too? What are you? STU—." Before he could get his last word out, I punched him in the gut as hard as I could.

He immediately began to cry and his friends ran over to pick him up. I looked them in the eyes and said, "Say another word to me, and I'll show you how much of a devil I am."

I learned that if I owned what they judged me for, I had nothing to fear. Even though I felt the shrapnel ripping deeper into my heart, I managed to conceal the pain behind a mask of rage. The crimson tempest of rage did not rampage or destroy blindly; I had mastered the storm within. With laser precision I poured its power into the goal of becoming stronger. I started to work harder than I ever did before. I needed to be number one in my class. I needed to be smarter than everyone else. I needed to be faster than everyone else; I needed to be better than what everyone told me I was. I wanted to be the best so that everyone would have no choice but to acknowledge that I was alive. I wanted them to acknowledge my worth, I wanted him to acknowledge my worth.

A Brief Glimmer of Hope:

Although my parents had initiated their divorce, my father still lived in the house. In my heart I held onto the hope that he would never leave; I wanted to believe that all would return to normal.

After the school year ended, my family made our annual trip to visit my grandmother in Florida. We would spend 16-20 hours in the car driving to get there from New York and we would only make two to three stops for maximum efficiency. I normally dreaded being in the car that long, but this year I was grateful. I happily put on my seatbelt as we departed because both my mother and father were in the car. I had thought that maybe "divorce" was just a word that parents said when they were angry at each other. I honestly believed that we would be returning to normalcy and that everything was going to be okay.

We eventually arrived to my grandmother's house, my father's mother, and all was okay in the world. My brother and I sat in the living room watching television as I laid sprawled out on the big, blue reclining chair. I had never felt so relieved, but that feeling faded fast when I started to hear yelling from the kitchen.

I watched as my mother stormed out of the kitchen, with my grandmother close on her heels. In confusion, I watched my grandmother pin my mom against the wall. She started calling out to my father. My mother called for my aunt, my father's sister, to "take the boys into another room, NOW!"

My aunt grabbed me as I tried to charge towards my mother. She brought Matthew and I into the bedroom. My brother was hysterically crying and I was frantic. My heart was pounding harder than it ever had in my entire life. Overcome with nausea and anxiety, I felt that I was going to vomit. My aunt crouched down to be eye level with us, "Your parents are getting a divorce, and this is normal. It is important for you to know that you can choose to live with your father if you wanted to."

In anger I shouted at her, "WHAT?! I don't want to choose! I want to see what's happening to mom! Why did Grandma grab her?! What's happening?!"

She immediately retorted, "don't you dare raise your voice to me boy!". Matthew started crying even harder. In that moment, she let go of my arm and grabbed him with both arms trying to calm him down. I saw my opportunity and took it. I cut to the right of her and bolted for the door. I scrambled to unlock it and ran out. As she made a move for me, Matthew screamed, "STOP!" When he did that, he bought me the extra second I needed to open the door. I ran to the other side of the house where all the yelling was happening. I ran across the living room, stumbling, but determined to see the truth with my own eyes. The living room never seemed so vast to me. What normally took seconds to cross felt like minutes.

Finally, I reached the other side of the corridor and I stood frozen in shock as I saw my father hurting my mother. I tried to yell, I tried to call for help, but the words wouldn't come out. All that came were the tears that I had thought left for good. Shaking with fear, I tried to force my words out, but my body wouldn't listen to me. On the inside I was screaming, "STOP! PLEASE STOP!" Yet, all I could manage was the faintest whisper. I started to step forward, but I was suddenly grabbed from behind. I was wrapped tightly in someone's arms as they tried to cover my eyes. I desperately pried at their fingers to see again. When I peeked through the cracks, I still saw the same nightmarish reality.

You may understand heartbreak, but have you ever experienced despair? My heart was already broken, but that night broke my soul. I was powerless to do anything but watch in horror as my family was torn apart by the same hands that put it together. In a way, I died that night. Hope? Love?

Warmth? No, I had no need for such things anymore. In the first breath of my new life, I realized that I was no longer that naive boy.

When I pulled together the pieces of my broken soul, I was reborn as the vessel of wrath. The only warmth left inside me could be found in my fury.

What happened after that? I honestly couldn't tell you. It is either so deeply repressed in my subconscious that my own mind has blocked it out trying to protect me or I simply blacked out. Later that same night, my father, mother, and older brother, drove back to New York. My little brother and I were left behind to stay for two weeks. This was the inaugural session of what I would later refer to as my annual two weeks of isolation and interrogation.

They may choose to argue that I had fun when I was there because we went to amusement parks, but I saw what it all really was, a dirty bribe. Unfortunately, my loyalty cannot be bought and my principles cannot be corrupted. I couldn't care less about what any of them did for me or whatever gifts they bought. *They were all dead to me* and there was absolutely nothing that they could do to ever regain my love. They tried to reinforce the idea that I didn't have to live with my mother, that, "I could see grandma every day if I chose to live with my father." Fueled with an ice-cold anger, I said, "I could truly care less if I ever saw any of you again." I was greeted with an immediate response of anger, "how dare you! . . ." It was all background noise to me, I had utterly detached from them all. At that point I thought that until the day that I die, I will never consider them my family.

At the end of the two longest weeks of my life, I was finally home in New York. I hugged my mom as hard as I could. I was so happy to see her again. We went to our room to unpack our bags and my mother tried to point out our gifts with excitement, "Look what grandma gave you, how nice!"

I thought to myself *"How are you acting like nothing has happened? Are we really just going to pretend?"*

I told her, "I don't want any of it, throw it all out." She looked at me perplexed, "But it's all new Ethan, are you sure you don't want it?" I repeated myself with greater intention, **"I don't want any of it. I don't care if it is new. I don't want anything that they gave me."**

In reflection, *that night* was the night that everything changed. The faintest glimmer of hope that I saw was nothing more than a trick of the light. We had truly come to the end of the line and there was no going back.

Comfortably Numb:

Despite my efforts over many years, my father never gave me the affirmation I needed. I was constantly belittled and had my successes undermined.

"Yeah, when I was your age, I did even better in school. I had even more awards than you," he said.

"Well, Dad, I am among the top in my class for high school. This week I had the highest scores on all my tests," I said.

"Ethan, your high school had a 60% graduation rate last year. It isn't difficult to stand out amongst a bunch of idiots."

I felt my blood boil as a white-hot anger climbed out of its cage and clawed its way out. My eyes narrowed and my jaw locked up.

"What, do you want to hit me? Do it. See what happens to you." His lips curled into a taunting smile, that infuriated me further.

I stood there and played out every possible scenario. *"I'm not as helpless as I was back then, I can fight this time."*

I looked at my little brother and he was tense; this was just a typical Sunday morning breakfast. With every word his venom would slither deeper into the corners of my mind. They pulled me under into the depths of sorrow and rage. I was never the type of person that cried outwardly though. I bottled away every tear deep inside me, convinced that if I even let one slide down my cheek, I would have been admitting defeat.

This wasn't done out of some macho ethos of masculinity, but out of survival. If a drop of blood falls into the water, the sharks are bound to come.

My brother was also angry, but he was scared, so I bit my lip as he continued to insult me. I savored the familiar taste of iron on my tongue, *"how many more times would I have to endure this metallic misery?"* The iron crawled down my throat and drowned the flames of my rage. My jaw loosened and my shoulders dropped.

He smiled malevolently, "That is what I thought."

He continued to tell me where all my shortcomings as a person were, but my eyes glazed over. I let go of my attachment to that moment, to him, to everyone, to everything. I let the ice kiss my tears and soothe my pain. I felt no pain, I felt no anger, I felt no warmth; *I was simply, perfectly, comfortably numb.*

When I detached, I would hide within myself. It was like being on autopilot. I would nod my head and words would leave my mouth, but they were all reflexive. Inside my mind I would see myself. The one inside my mind was possessed with rage. I would walk up to him, and say,

"Don't let him win."

"Everything, will be fine."

"You are strong."

"You are in control."

"You are worth loving."

"You are smart."

"You *will* prove them all wrong"

That part of me would begin to cry, uncontrollably. He would plead with me choking on his own tears, "How? How do we win? Will the pain ever stop?"

I spoke to him, "Our tears are ours and ours alone. If you need to cry, do it in here. You have seen what happens when you put your faith in others? They hurt you, they hurt us. We will survive, and we will be free, because there are no other options."

Reflection:

At this point in my life, my heart was shattered. The pain had been overwhelming to me and there were times when I thought about ending my life. However, inside of me, there was always my voice of rebellion. In the depths of my despair, I had taught myself how to detach. When I stared into the mirror and faced my mortality, I realized that I was afraid to die. I wasn't ready to leave this world, so I started conditioning my mind to fight back.

When I was 12 years old, I learned how to meditate. I am convinced that this saved my life. I would sit cross-legged with my back against the wall. Once in position, I would allow my eyes to close and I would listen to the instrumental music playing in my ear buds. In my mind I would envision the number 20. I would change its structure, size, and color. Then, I would begin counting down as I took deep breaths. My chest would inflate and I would hold the warmth inside of me. If I grew distracted in my countdown, I would revert to 20 and would start the process again.

My desired state of relaxation was accompanied with a sensation of falling. In an instant I would feel my body drop and I could really hear myself think. In the peak of my relaxation, I would start rewiring my mind to think in more positive terms. In order to conquer my self-doubt and depression, I would practice shifting my perspective. I would watch the words that others used to describe me evaporate off my body and fade into nothingness. I began writing words of my own onto my skin. I chose to define myself. When I shifted my perspective, it was not with the programming, "Life could be worse." Instead I taught myself:

"Life could be amazing."

Although our hearts may break, they can also heal. *Did you know that when a bone breaks, it rebuilds itself stronger than before?* I like to think of my heart in those terms. In time, the fractures in my heart would close. I too would become stronger than before.

Believe in your heart and its ability to heal. Although we may break, do not allow yourself to stay broken. You do not need to learn to love again, because you have never forgotten. How can you forget the one thing that is innate to humanity?

In order to give love, we must first love ourselves.

Chapter 4
THE WOLF

The Wolf
by Ethan DeAbreu

I'm not hungry
I'm ravenous
I'm starving
My appetite is insatiable

Only sheep wait to be fed
I have no Shepard
I am untamed
I will eat my fill

Never satisfied
Always wolfish

Do you know what the difference between a black sheep and a lone wolf is? Have you ever considered that they were different in the first place? There was a point in my life when I had convinced myself that I was the black sheep in the herd. My mind was never wired quite like other people, although, it was perpetually wired. At night, I would play mental games of catch, where I would throw my thoughts against the four walls of my cluttered mind and would see what bounced back. I was always filled with questions and they would often get me into trouble. My teachers would find my questions cumbersome and my peers could never understand why I thought those things.

I was never satisfied with one-word answers. I wanted an explanation, a story.

Up until the fourth grade, I attended a private religious school.

Today, while I don't identify as a religious person, I can appreciate that at every religion's core they try to communicate a message of love, peace, and understanding. Unfortunately, that message is often lost due to the interpretations and motives of people. The actions of an individual do not speak for the whole. It is important that you understand this before I tell you this story.

At the time, I was about nine years old and I was already struggling with my concept of God. My parents began their divorce two years earlier, only a few weeks after I made my Holy Communion. No matter how much I cried and prayed at night, nothing changed. I was powerless and I could not stop my world from crumbling down around me. After what felt like decades of warfare in my home, there was a momentary cease fire. The divorce was settled and one day when I came home, my father was gone. He actually took my dog too. I didn't even get a chance to say goodbye. Without warning, two of the things that I loved most in the world were gone. Fortunately, my heart was already broken at that point, so it couldn't be broken again. *Who cares if someone stomps on broken glass?* The damage was already done.

This story begins in my world history class. I always found history to be fascinating because it seemed like the people from those times lived in a completely different world from modern people. However, as I grew older, I realized nothing has really changed. Although technology has advanced, there are people in the world that make me believe that we have devolved as a species. We have been fighting the same old wars led by the same old demagogues. We are in a perpetual state confrontation with each other because of the circumstances of our birth and upbringing.

We are constantly battling between fact and belief, between hope and fear, between white and colored, and between poor and rich. We as a species choose profits over people; we choose to look the other way rather than addressing the true evils in the world. We believe we can do nothing and that someone else will "deal" with it. If ignorance is not a sufficient excuse for breaking the law, it shouldn't be one for allowing children to starve to death, for people to be sold into slavery, and the oppression of our most basic human rights. Ignorance is not blissful, it's shameful. We need to be constantly asking ourselves how we can do more.

As I type these words, I remember the history lesson that changed my perception of the world. We were given a few minutes to read a passage from the textbook and then we would discuss what we read. My appetite for these stories was voracious. As I finished the passage, I turned the page to keep reading and I read something that lead to a major realization in my life. I read that approximately six-million Jews perished in the Holocaust. I sat there for a moment and tried to understand what I just read. I knew how much six million was. That was one hundred thousand sixty times. It was ten thousand six hundred times! In my head the questions were flooding my mind, "Six million? SIX MILLION?!" "Why?

Why?! Why would people do something so horrible . . . Why didn't God help them?"

As you can imagine, the combination of the nature of that loaded question and my curious mind trying to make sense of the most horrific thing I had ever read in my life got me into a lot of trouble. In my naivety, I asked the question that roared in my mind without much hesitation, "Six million . . . is a lot of people. . . why didn't God help them? How could he not help them?"

The other kids actually stirred in their seats a bit asking each other the same question. I saw my teacher's face tighten and with great difficulty she said, "Well, they prayed to a different God, from a different religion." I immediately asked another question, "There are other religions?! How many are there?" She didn't answer me. I asked another question, "How are there other religions when there is only one God?" I ask another without getting an answer for the first three, "why didn't their God save them?" Another one, "Why didn't our God save them? We are all his children after all?" "ENOUGH!" She retorted. "take your seat at once, and only speak when called upon!"

The other kids started to laugh, but I was so confused. I didn't understand what was wrong with my question. I started mumbling to myself, "but . . .I don't understand. . ."

My teacher heard me, "One more peep out of you, and you'll go straight to the principal's office!" I sank into my seat, still lost in thought. I was only slightly distracted by the other students laughing at me getting into trouble. In that moment, my anger started to seethe out of me and I realized why I was different from the other kids. The difference was that I had questions while they accepted what they were told.

The difference between the black sheep and the lone wolf is choice. The black sheep is ostracized by the herd because he is born inherently different from them. The lone wolf, however, breaks away from the pack because of his actions. I am speaking in the colloquial sense of the terms and not to testify whether or not this actually happens in nature. For so long I tried to close my eyes and pretend that I was a part of their herd, but I was only disillusioning myself. I couldn't go on accepting that someone was going to form my beliefs, values, and thoughts.

As I sucked air in, I felt the snarl of the wolf in the roof of my mouth. The breath of the wild filled my lungs as I howled for freedom.

How ridiculous. I was a wolf that tried to pleat like the sheep. For so long I feared the animosity of the herd, but the only thing more ridiculous than a pleating wolf is a sheep baring its teeth to one.

There Are No Negotiations Between Wolves and Sheep.

If someone told you to close your eyes while you were driving a car, would you trust them? What if it was important to the other person that you did? It is the most important thing in the world to this other person. If you did not do this one thing for them, you would really be letting them down. Would you do it, and if you did, would you peek?

The answer to this question should always be "no." You would have to be some sort of lunatic to drive on any road with your eyes closed. If you hesitate to come to that answer, that means you are ignoring what is painfully apparent in order to satisfy someone else's needs.

How often do we live our lives for someone else? How often do we accept the dogma of others in order to stay in line with the norm? As human beings, we are not one size fits all pieces. Each and every one of us has their own unique shape, but we sacrifice our individuality for acceptance. That is what society has conditioned us to do.

I imagine every person as having their own fluid shape and color. Can you see yours? Close your eyes and tell me, what is the color of your soul? It may seem silly, believe me, I understand cynicism. However, you picked this book up for a reason. You wanted to change, so for that part of you that craved something new. . . try to see the color of your soul. If you cannot find it, go look for it.

That color is representative of your true nature. There is a reason why it appealed to you. It is so much more than a shade or a tint of a primary color; this color is something innate to you. When I imagine the color of my soul, I see a rich azure blue like the midnight sky that fills the canopy of my mind. As I look within, I get lost in the riddles of the world. I have always imagined this color to be mysterious and alluring. The midnight sky is silent and peaceful, yet it always present and immensely powerful. I have never forgotten the color of my soul, because it is a precious element of myself. Although the external world may try to force you into a box made of black steel and try to steal your color and shape, you will never forget it. You see, we never truly forget the intimate parts of ourselves. We just choose to ignore them.

Like an animal trapped in a cage, our true colors thrash against the walls of the boxes we put them in. However, they eventually they get tired of fighting back. They are exhausted and their resolve has been broken by the perpetual self-indulgent ignorance we thrive on. We acquire Stockholm Syndrome of the soul; we disillusion ourselves into believing that this is what we always wanted. We try to convince ourselves and others with incessant Facebook posts, Instagram photos, and Snapchats that we are satisfied with the choices we made. However, our hearts will always know the truth. Crippled by the fear of being left behind by everyone else, we mindlessly follow. That's all that seems to matter to us anymore: followers, hearts, likes, and retweets. We will take all the validation we can get, but never question the worth of the source.

True validation can never come from an external source; the greatest validation we can achieve in this lifetime is the realization of our dreams. Instead of counting such frivolous metrics of mediocrity; start counting: the number of calories you burned at the gym, the number of books you have read, and the number of lives you have left an impact on.

The harsh truth is that if you spend your life more concerned with what others think of you, rather than what you think of yourself, you will find nothing, but mediocrity and misery.

Back in that classroom, I made the choice to live my life searching for the answers to the questions that burn inside of me. I decided to walk away from the life that everyone else was so convinced that I should be living. I chose to walk towards the question that scared me the most:

"... Exactly ... how different am I?"

The Wolf's Path

To deliberately choose to be alone seems counter intuitive to human nature; we are social creatures. The idea of being alone may even seem daunting to some. However, I had no choice, I needed to learn how to be comfortable with myself. Shortly after my previous realization about myself, I had changed schools, and another five times after that. Loneliness comes with the territory of being the new kid in school. While some are allured to the mystery of someone new, others are threatened by it. I seemed to have a talent for attracting bullies or just trouble for that matter. In school I would be bullied for being smart and at my father's house I would be ridiculed for my stupidity. Even in my youth, my dark sense of humor could appreciate the painful irony in that.

As the fangs of loneliness sink deep into the fibers of the heart, its venom seeps into the cracks staining it black like frostbite. You can either grow numb to the pain or learn to love the cold. If you are not careful the toxicity can devour you from the inside out, but if you choose to survive, the venom becomes the vaccination. With each inoculation, you will slowly build an immunity to the toxicity and realize that the pain was what was making you stronger.

As a result, I no longer fear loneliness. It was a bitter medicine, but as always, the best ones always are the worst tasting. In my solitude, I realized that the most important form of acceptance that can be achieved is self-acceptance. We often become our own worst enemy when we start accepting the negative perceptions of others as defining who we really are. However, when your voice is the only voice, it allows you to think clearly. At one point, I felt hated by everyone. I was unwelcome and unwanted. I honestly believed there was no place for me in the world. It did not matter if I was at school or at home, someone was always reminding me how stupid and worthless I was. I'm not sure if you have ever felt "worthlessness" before, but to those who understand the depth of the word, you know the feeling. It's like you have a black hole in the center of your chest. Every intimate thought, everything you love, and everything you hate; is all is consumed and crushed under the gravity of the feeling. You lose everything that ever defined you, even your name bears no meaning to you. When you walk in a crowd, you are aware of the inevitability of your destruction, just as the black hole has consumed everything else.

The hunger won't be satisfied until you too are devoured. Inside the black hole you are not dead, but it feels as if you are. That is true loneliness. I stayed in that place for so long. Each day I was being crushed by the weight of my burdens, but those on the outside world didn't even notice. *How did I escape?* I simply walked out of it . . .

I freed myself by embracing my loneliness. I accepted it as a part of me and in doing so I accepted myself. I came to the understanding that those people were on the outside world for a reason. These people should have no significant impact on my internal world. I started living my life in accordance to the thought, "It doesn't matter if people don't agree with my decisions, or accept me; at the end of the day, all that matters is that I respect myself." As I walked out of the void, I left all the negativity within. In desolation I found my peace; I learned how to stand tall while carrying the weight of my burdens on my back.

Finding Your Pack

When you no longer crave acceptance from others, it presents you with opportunity to make friends that accept you for who you really are. Your real friends don't care about how much money you have and what kind of clothes you wear. They won't pressure you into making damaging decisions because "it would be fun."

I never searched for the friends I have today. They found me. My best friends found me because we shared the same values and they saw that I actively lived life on my terms. The day came for this lone wolf to find his new pack and I am certainly better off for it. I stopped associating myself with sheep and found the wolves. I mean, some of my friends are vegan; however, they all had that same look in their eyes. They have that insatiable hunger for more. They dared to question their environments and the motivations of others. As a result, they freed themselves from mediocrity.

The Wolf's path is my path. It doesn't have to be yours. I don't mind if you scoff at me or think it's funny. If you did, it just shows that you don't understand. As I said earlier, it is not my objective to have people understand me; I want you to understand yourself. You may not relate to the creed of wolves...

The Jungle Book
by Rudyard Kipling

"Now this is the Law of the Jungle
As old, and as true as the sky;
And the wolf that shall keep it may prosper,
But the wolf that shall break it must die

> *As the creeper that girdles the tree trunk*
> *The Law runneth forward and back;*
> *For the strength of the pack is the wolf,*
> *And the strength of the wolf is the pack."*

Perhaps there is a different creed that calls to you, but that is for you to determine on your own. There is more than one path to freedom, but you will not find it if you are concerned with what everyone else is doing. The circumstances of your birth should not dictate your path. However, if you choose to surrender yourself to the frivolous, they shall own you. We are much smarter than sheep and we should always question the dogma that we are being fed. Do not accept things as they are merely because that is the way they have always been. Do not accept things at face value. Just because someone said something was true, that doesn't mean that it was.

Train your mind to question all things, especially hatred, because hatred is born of ignorance. Choosing to hate something is choosing to be ignorant to love. In my eyes, I do not acknowledge those who claim to be black sheep. Sheep are sheep and wolves are wolves. Just as they are the same species, we as humanity, are the same species; the only thing that divides us is *choice*.

The blind hatred that runs rampant in our world is a by-product of intentional ignorance to the absolute law that, we as humanity, regardless of skin color, race, wealth, or religion, are one and the same. We have allowed ourselves to become divided by standards of the imaginary. We have been fooled into hating those who do not share the same beliefs as us. We have been duped to believe that meaningful peace can only be achieved through war.

In our folly we act as fools do, oblivious to our surroundings. We dismiss the responsibility for the suffering of our people and choose to believe the narrative that we were helpless to make a difference. We say things like "there are children starving in Africa" lightly, as a means to tease others for not finishing their food. Although it may seem like a harmless joke on one end, it is a stark reality on the other.

The only course of action to combat ignorance is to seek enlightenment. Start questioning the world around you and your place in it. Learn how to form your own original opinions and thoughts. I like to employ the concept of "tabula rasa" when I approach a new idea. If we are born as blank slates, then can't we become what we once were again? I empty my mind and dispose of any previous opinions of something when I wish to truly understand it. If you go into something new already deciding on how you feel, you will learn nothing. I understand that I was born ignorant to the ways of the world, but I will actively seek understanding until the day that I perish. Don't live your lives following the will of another, because at the end of it all, you will die, asking the one question:

"Did I ever find purpose in life?"

I am not a sheep waiting for my Shepherd to lead me to my meal. I am a wolf that walks amongst sheep. With teeth bared, I will bite down, until I draw blood from the hand that tries to feed me. I am wild and untamed. I will eat or starve at my own accord, but that is the price for knowing the truth. You may not be one of my pack. If that is the case, I recommend you stay out of my path. Afterall, there are no negotiations between wolves and sheep. You can choose blissful ignorance, but be prepared to be lead to the slaughter by the hand that feeds you. I refuse to stand idly by while this happens. *Although I may not have the might of the majority, I would much rather have the right of the minority. If you follow the masses you will never see what lies ahead.*

The world we live in can change if we take an interest in the future. Alone we may not be able to make a large impact. However, if we band together, we are not so helpless. We must embody the changes we wish to see in this world. There is no such thing as being too young to be involved in your own future. Wisdom is not achieved through age, but rather through experience. Fill your lives with unique and interesting experiences in order to come to your own conclusions. Remember that nothing is guaranteed on your journey. More often than not, the path to enlightenment is a lonely one. Although that may seem daunting, it is because many turn a blind eye to the path because of their fear. Will you allow your mind and destiny to be ruled by fear? Or will you summon the courage that is within you to walk away?

Chapter 5
L**IMIT** B**REAKER**

Clouds of uncertainty loom overhead and doubt takes shelter in the corners of my mind. I face the approaching storm as my spirit is gusted away by the winds. I find myself shivering uncontrollably as the storm breathes malevolence. I'm overwhelmed and outmatched.

What am I to do?

How many times must I endure the ferocity of the storm?

Some days when I wake up, it's like a monster is standing on my back. I can feel its claws tearing into my flesh like an anchor being dragged across the ocean floor. I can feel the weight of it pulling me deeper into the depths of my doubts in my Socratic Hell of "what ifs and whys."

As I close my eyes, it is like I am just letting go. The pain of the weight begins to subside as I stop putting up resistance. I allow the numbing mist of darkness to swallow and devour me along with the pain that I carry inside.

Perhaps, this is freedom?

Rebirth After Ruin

At the ripe age of twelve I reached my breaking point. This was the first time that I ever considered taking my own life. I had just come home from a weekend at my father's and I was mentally and spiritually exhausted. Like a succubus, that house sapped me of every ounce of life and left me teetering on the edge of death. I was so tired of having to be driven from New Jersey to New York for two and a half hours just so that I could be berated for 48 hours. I had been struggling to make friends at my new school, but I lied to my father about how well I was doing. I told him, "Dad, I did the best in my class on this test! I'm doing really well, everyone thinks I'm smart."

Whereas, in reality, I would do anything possible to get me out of going to school. I was bullied relentlessly; I was rejected by the other students for hanging out with a kid they didn't like. I had gotten into several fights in and out of school, but no matter how many times I would win, there would still be a way for me to lose. The teachers didn't believe me when I told them what was wrong and who was bullying me because they were all "such good kids." They were great at playing the game and posing at the right moments. Furthermore, they were ruthless. If they couldn't get to me, they would get to my little brother. They knew that hurt the most.

My father made it a point to break through my little charade, "Well, Ethan, when you line up ten idiots and pick the smartest of those idiots, what are you left with?"

I glared at him and the anger seethed out of my eyes like red smoke.

"Don't look at me like that boy and answer the question."

Gritting my teeth, I begrudgingly answered his question, "the smartest idiot..."

I excused myself from the table and went upstairs to "shower." As the floorboards creaked and splintered beneath my feet, I could feel my mask of strength do the same thing. I quickly turned on the shower and began to cry uncontrollably. With cupped hands, I covered my mouth to mask the sounds. When I felt myself losing control over how loud I was crying I would bite down on the knuckle of my index finger to calm down . . . it was a different kind of pain, but I would rather feel that.

As I lie on my back, defeated, the storm mocked,
"Why do you even bother, you're worthless after all?"
"You're too stupid to make a difference."
"You're too ugly for anyone to love."
"There is nothing special about you,"
"Everyone hates you."
"It would be better, if you just died."

I started to think, "they are all right about me. I really am just worthless. The world would probably be better off without me."

It was honestly no different than any of the other weekends that I had spent there, but today, I just couldn't keep it together anymore. Ever since they divorced, I had tried my best to put on a strong face for my mom and brother. I also couldn't show any weakness to the outside world because rather than help me when I had fallen, they spat at my misfortune. Although I tried to project confidence to the world, I felt like I was imploding.

The weekend had come and passed and after another two and half hours I was back in my bedroom. Tomorrow it was Monday. . . back to school. The feeling of dread was pouring over me and I felt a cold sweat come over me. I went downstairs and I grabbed a knife out of the drawer. Then I quietly returned to my room and locked my door. As I sat on my bed, I stared at the knife in my hand and fell into a deep trance. As I followed the edge of the knife with my finger, I saw a blurred reflection of myself in the metal. I cynically smiled to myself and said, "that's all that's left, I don't even recognize myself anymore."

My demons were perched on my back, digging their claws deeper into my shoulders as they took a tighter grasp of me. My eyes were swollen and heavy; I hadn't enjoyed a good night of sleep for what felt like years. Just as I dreamt vividly, my nightmares were just as vivid and crippling. There was no break from the torture; even in my dreams I felt unwelcome and haunted.

When I faced myself, it was like watching a recording of my life with all of these different people sending the same message: "you're worthless."

I grasped the knife even tighter in my hand and brought it towards my arm. However, the rebellious part in my soul wouldn't allow me to commit. I cried as I clutched the knife tighter, my knuckles turning white in my grasp. I just couldn't do it. Frustrated, and at my breaking point, I felt my rage smother my sorrow.

I threw the knife across my room and said,

"NO! I am tired of feeling like this! I have had enough! I need to change, I need to be better. I am a survivor, I have always found a way and I am not giving up now or ever again! It's not a mask, you are strong. I can do this, I've always had to fight and I'm not done yet."

There I was again, in the eye of the storm. As I looked up I saw a thread of light escape the maelstrom. I watched attentively as it fell towards me like a feather, delicately swaying from side to side, carried by a gentle breeze.

The light landed on the center of my chest like a tender kiss. I was tired of feeling this way and I decided to change. As I tugged at the thread of light that reached me, I watched in wonder as the storm fell apart at the seams. As I climbed out of the hole that I found my way into, the storm spiraled and shrank until it sat in the palm of my hand. I then put it in a glass bottle and sealed it with a cork.

I watched as the tempest surged within the bottle, slamming against the walls of its confinement in defiance. I apologized, with a smile on my face,

"I'm sorry, but I cannot allow to control me anymore. Don't worry, I'm not going to throw you away or abandon you so that someone else can find you. You are a part of me and I accept that. However, rather than allowing you to beat me down, I'm going to use you as my fuel."

Those words you said before are not my words, so they have no right to try and define me. That privilege belongs to me and me alone. I have value and I will spend my days searching for my place in the world. There is a place for me; I can make a difference.

The storm can either be our greatest foe or our most powerful weapon.

When you have a dream, you must protect it from doubt. It seems that many of us have been deceived; we have come to mistake the voice in our ear for the voice in our head. We have been fed a narrative that leads us to believe that we are inadequate. However, you were not born into this world to live to the expectations of others. You have to learn how to identify the source of the pain and then *let go*.

I know suicide is a strange thing to read about or talk about in our culture. It feels even weirder writing about it. However, it is an important conversation to be had. It seems that we only talk about it when it is already too late. It was very difficult for me to vocalize these feelings to you in my words. I have never spoken about it with another person. I know that so many of you out there are in pain and you are struggling to find meaning. There is meaning, we just have to fight to create it. The cruel irony about life is that we only realize how precious it is when we approach the end. As I faced the reality of my death, I decided that my life does have value and regardless of what other people thought of me, I was going to live. This life was given to me and nobody else; only I have the right to say what it's worth. I faced the younger version of myself, the one that would go to the backyard and cry every day after school. I told him that everything was going to be okay and that we made the right choice. Now it was time to see things through. It was time to dust myself off and start fighting back, because that is the only thing I ever really known how to do.

"They don't want to acknowledge me? They think I'm a failure? I'll prove them wrong and they will have no choice but to see what I have accomplished!"

The Greatest Power is One You Give:

What the world could always use more of is empathy. People need to learn to see with more than just your eyes.

If you look carefully at another person, passed the layers of the superficial we hide underneath, you will see the person who is really there. In my experience, once you dig deep enough, you will see another person no different from you. We are the same: we have fears, we have dreams, we have doubt, we have love and hatred. However, we all reach different paths based off of the experiences we have had along the way. Everyone has a battle they are facing and a piece of themselves they want to overcome. If, however, fear takes the reins, people become lost. Loneliness is a difficult burden to bear; it may not always show on the surface, but on the inside, it tears a person apart. Reach out to others with kindness and warmth. Always stand up for what is right and remember that you are never alone. Who knows, maybe you could even save a life. It doesn't take much to be a hero, sometimes it just starts with a hello and a smile.

Writing My Story:

I like to think of myself as the protagonist in my own story that is on his hero's journey. We have all seen these great stories where we watch an ordinary person become a hero. Whether if it is in a book or at a movie, it inspires us and touches our hearts. It is the story of the person who kept going in the most difficult of times and in the process made great friends, learned about themselves, and finally understood what they were truly capable of. Some stories resonate with us more than others and it leads us to wonder, *"what if I worked a little harder? Could I be like them?"*

I grew tired of being the spectator, so I left the crowd and embarked on my own journey. It may seem strange to others and I know that a lot of people will misunderstand me along the way. Roadblocks? Failures? Heartache? Lost friends? All of those things are inevitable on the path to fulfil your personal legend. However, fate can be kind to those who are bold enough to go searching for it. Although you may have to endure the storm; it's all a test of your grit. Did you think it would be easy? Did you have the perfect plan, but then it all fell apart? If you gave up when you reached your first roadblock, then maybe you weren't watching the movie as closely as you should have been. Nothing ever goes according to plan. When you reach conflict, you should know by now that this is the rising action leading to the pinnacle of your adventure! You can't give up your quest when the story just starts to get interesting; this is the part when you do something witty and creative that gets you out of a dire situation. You dig deep into the well of your soul and pull out a new strength that you never realized you had. Without conflict you can't have a story.

When you come face to face with your limits, you can either choose to accept them for what they are or smash through the walls that dared to tell you where your journey ended. It isn't over until you say it is over.

In order to conquer the limits that I set on myself, I decided to start filling my mind with positive things and learning. I decided to turn my attention to my hero for advice. I had admired him for both his incredible martial arts skills and his philosophy. Although I will never have the chance to speak to him in person, I researched his interviews and soaked in every word he said. Every hero has a teacher,

> *"If you always put limit on everything you do, physical or anything else. It will spread into your work and into*

your life. There are no limits. There are only plateaus, and you must not stay there, you must go beyond them."

-Bruce Lee

Take a moment and sit with that.

What that quote taught me was that mentality and your perception of the world is what holds the power to save yourself. I realized that this low point was merely a plateau and not rock bottom. I had climbed from the lowest I have been and as long as I kept my eyes ahead, I would survive. I decided to start making those steps in the right direction to improve myself. If I started to believe that change was possible, then I at least stood a chance of creating it.

While on the path to self-improvement it is important to be weary of who you surround yourself with. More often than not, the words that hurt us the most come from the people that we love the most. The people we are closest to can have a significant impact on our views of what is possible and what we are capable of. Within the past year, three people that I cared very deeply about, betrayed my love with words that carried catastrophic consequences. I nearly betrayed my love by assigning any value to it.

Perhaps the most devastating one came from the person that I considered as a brother. I had been working on project in my senior year of college where I would use media platforms to provide people with motivation and advice. I was really excited to start the project because a significant amount of planning had gone into it. I wanted to make a difference. Many people greeted it with positivity. However, one of the opinions that mattered most to me, stomped down on my heart.

"Ethan, what makes you think that you are someone that has a right to talk about motivation? Do you consider yourself a leader? If so, why?"

I could not believe the words that were coming out of his mouth. I thought to myself, *"If you were truly my brother, you would know who I am. I shouldn't have to convince you of my worth."*

I calmly, but firmly responded to him, "It's not a matter of me considering myself to be a leader, because I am a leader. I operate in that capacity in both my personal and professional life. All I want to do is inspire people to keep going when they are ready to give up. I think I am qualified enough to do that."

As if to twist the dagger he already plunged in my heart, he said, "have you ever considered that you are not a leader, and that you just surround yourself with a *low caliber of people?* I go to a very prestigious college and what you are doing is not special; there are plenty of people better for the job than you. I go to school in order to be groomed for leadership and in my opinion, I don't think that you should be talking about it."

In anger, I turned off my phone, packed my bags, and drove to the gym. There have always been undertones of this negativity in him. However, I chose to ignore it because we have been friends for more than ten years. That was my mistake and I won't make it again.

The gym has always been a great tool for me to discharge my stress and anxiety in a productive way. I poured all the pain of this betrayal into the iron that surrounded me. With each repetition, I was detoxifying myself of the negativity of others. Their negativity is poison and it must be expelled. If it is not, it will erode your dreams and your confidence.

I have always been the type of person that simmers with his feelings for a while before I talk about it to anyone. In my mind, I slowly walked through the situation and what I was feeling.

"What he said hurt, but it wasn't the worst thing that anyone has ever said to you. Who cares who he was to you? This is not the first time that someone you trusted hurt you. There are always going to be people that put you down; people will always misunderstand a message, even if it is a good one. None of that matters. Let go of your anger. People have doubted you before and you know what? Who was right in the end?"

With a sense of resolution, I forgave him for the pain he caused me and accepted that no one but me will ever really understand what I am capable of. I started to let of go the doubts that I let bury me. I reflected on my past and realized that:

"I am the summation of what I think I am"

Our perception of ourselves is the most important thing for us to develop. When you tame your ego with humility, you can find understanding. When you silence your doubts, you can find peace.

I have spent an enormous amount of my time investing in my mind. After reading many books, watching many documentaries, and simply living life; I have developed a philosophy that endures through the most difficult of times.

The Philosophy of Mental Fortitude

Are we bodies with a mind? Or minds with a body? It's a strange thing to consider, but it is important to understand.

What I have come to realize is that my physical self is the manifestation of what I believed was possible for me. Our bodies move according to our will. As a result, if we discipline our minds, we can create our freedom. We must learn to become selective about what we allow to penetrate the membrane of our thoughts and become anti fragile to the thoughts that drag us into despair.

I started crafting fortifications for my mind through meditation when I was twelve. My love of martial arts had led me to study the greatest that ever were. I learned that martial artists all had practiced meditation in order to conquer their minds. These people were accredited with performing near superhuman feats and had created lifetimes filled with achievement. They inspired me to learn myself.

When I meditate, I allow my mind to drift somewhere far off. I close my eyes and the mental landscape of my mind takes me to the summit of a mountain. As I focus on my breath to center myself I can feel the icy chill of the air fill my lungs. I can feel the frosty kiss of the melting snow as it reaches the heat of my body. The contrasting forces remind me of the duality that exists within the world and myself. There is a piece of me that feels fear, doubt, and sadness; yet, there is another that feels ambition, pride, and tenacity. Both are important pieces to who I am and both exist in the same plain at the same time. While at the summit, I can sit alone with my thoughts and truly face myself. With each breath, I fall deeper into the heart of all things. I ask myself the hardest question in the world . . . *"why?"*

The first step to facing your problems is to ask yourself, "why it is a problem in the first place?" Then analyze the way it makes you feel: angry, anxious, sad, etc. You must get to the root of your emotions. You must truly understand yourself and your feelings. Once you reach the core of any emotion you can sift through the layers of excuses and qualifications and see the truth of the matter. The most hurtful lies we tell are the ones we tell ourselves.

Once you understand the truth of your emotions, you will be able to form your resolve. You must free yourself of the lies that protect your ego. Let go of the mirage that hides the true you and see what inspires you. Understand your resolve.

When I imagine my resolve, I see a wisp of blue flame burning in the center of my chest. The flame flickers with each heartbeat and takes root in my soul. My resolve does not allow me to drown in self-pity; it firmly commands me to save myself. Despite whatever downpour of hardship comes my way, I will not be extinguished. I will endure.

Mental fortitude is the philosophy that I created to help me understand my place in the world. My heart was filled to the brim with so much pain and I was drowning in it. I believed that I was worthless and with each day I went spiraling further down into the abyss. I thought all there was in life was misery and pain. I was tired of fighting, but I found a new path when I found the words:

"Life is suffering."

That is the first truth of Buddhism. When I read those words for the first time, I cried, because I felt that I understood their depth. The Buddha was not speaking in a tone of melancholy; the phrase was not to communicate that life was meaningless. Those words touched my soul. I understood that in this life suffering was inevitable. We are ephemeral, fading flickers of existence, and the awareness of our impermanence and dissatisfaction is suffering. However, just as life is impermanent, so are our circumstances. I learned that I didn't have to be what others told me that I was; *I could change*. The contemplation of life and suffering lead me to the thought,

"Strength is a choice."

We can either choose to suffer, or derive meaning from it. Although we may suffer, the pain is what makes us human, and how we respond to it will impact how we grow. Oddly enough, it is often those who endured the most pain that have the kindest hearts. Their exterior may be rough and hardened by the bouts of life, yet their hearts have a greater capacity to love. They have a better understanding of how to give love because they understand the pain of never receiving it.We spend too much of our lives waiting for someone to give us the power to save ourselves. That strength has always been inside of us; we simply needed the courage to ask it of ourselves. Embrace a mindset that empowers you when you feel defeated.

I believe in mental fortitude because it has taught me how to smile in the face of adversity. When others imposed limitations on me, it gave me the strength to strive pass them. It gave me resolve, when others doubted me. It taught me that suffering is inevitable, but how long I suffer is up to me. It gave me the courage to stand for what is right, even if it meant standing alone.

You are the protagonist of your own story and once you start to believe that, you can start writing what happens next. The only limits that exist are in the extent of your imagination and how far you are willing to go to pursue your dream.

Chapter 6
Dreams

I was always fascinated by the stars. They were magnificent orbs of hydrogen and helium that peer through the cloak of midnight, casting their fiery light upon the sleeping world. Although there were so many of them, I always imagined them to be lonely. I know this type of thinking is contradictory, but so many of our thoughts are of that nature.

I always wanted to reach the stars so that I could tell them how beautiful they were. I wanted to thank them for lighting up my world while the sun rested. I wanted to thank them for keeping me company as I sat alone pondering my thoughts and feelings.

I was determined that today would be the day I finally reached them. My world faded to black as my eyes fell shut. I inhaled and the icy winter air filled my lungs. I held my breath and let the sensation fill me. My mind was waiting for the opportune moment and then the wind whispered, "now." My eyes snapped open and I began sprinting with my target in sight. This time I was going to succeed, this time for sure. As the stamina evaporated out of me, I made a desperate leap towards the sky and snatched at it. As I fell to the ground, I tightly clenched my fist. Laying on my back, I opened my hand. In it were the twisting shadows of the midnight around me. In other words, they were empty. Yet again, I had failed to grasp a star out of the sky. Although slightly vexed by my failure, I was not yet defeated. I lay on the ground looking at the ever-elusive wonder before me and smiled. Although today I did not manage to take a star from the sky, there was always tomorrow. My success was inevitable.

When we are young, our imagination is boundless. We didn't understand what it meant to be realistic; we only saw possibility. The ability to dream and ponder the impossible is the most magnificent thing about being human. Yet, as we age, we tend to suppress our gift.

In John Locke's *Essay Concerning Human Understanding*, he introduces the concept of "tabula rasa" or blank slate. Essentially, he asserts that when we are born, we are born without the imprints of experience and society. In time, the philosophies of others are etched and hammered into our smooth surface. With each strike and motion we become something further away from what we originally were.

Change is an imperative component of growth. However, the mechanism of our development is important to assess. Are you changing because of something you desire? Or for what someone desires for you? If you reflect upon that, perhaps you will see that other people have been trying to sculpt the future *they* deemed *best* for you. First it was your parents, then your teachers, your professors, your boss; it seems as if everyone wants to tell you what is best for you. Although some of those people may sincerely have your best interests at heart, it does not mean that they are right in their assumptions.

Our parents, although they may mean well, often feed us an ethos that cripples us. They teach us to associate uncertainty with failure because of their fears. Try to imagine your parent at your age and what was going through their minds. Maybe they had a dream too, maybe it was similar to yours. Take a look around. Every single person on this planet had a dream at some point, but many grow bitter and end up being defeated in time. There may have been a point in time when they believed in the vitality of their dreams, but they slowly substituted their dreams for "reality." They put their passion on the back burner in order to get a job. When a person lets go of their dream, they are letting go of their optimism and their youth. Your parents may understand the pain of letting go of a dream and they try to protect you from feeling the same pain by discouraging you.

When I speak with my mom, it becomes clear to me that she has locked away her youthful dreams in order to face reality. My mother gave up everything to move to the United States from Singapore, in order to live with my father. She had a dream of having a family with the man that she loved and spending the rest of her days in marital bliss. However, when she came to the states, she was met with a different reality. My father was not the man that he had been in Singapore and in time abuse became a daily reality for my mother. I understand her heart. When she warns me about my ideas and passions, she is trying to protect me from having my dreams turning into my nightmares.

On the other hand, my father attacked my self-worth as a child. I was always struggling with the idea of my self-worth and if I had any worth at all. He made me feel that I was not good enough to achieve any task, let alone the things I dreamt of. As I have aged, I don't feel as much anger for my father as I once did. A part of me understands where his resentment came from. I understand that what he said to me was a projection of what he was feeling. He met my excitement with spite because he saw a piece of himself that discarded a long time ago in my eyes. To let go of your dreams is one thing, but to have a daily reminder that they were once there, that must have been difficult.

If we spend the rest of our lives waiting for someone else to believe in our dreams to give us the confidence to go pursue them, we could be waiting forever.

I often reflect upon a quote from *The Alchemist*, written by one of my favorite authors Paulo Coelho,

> **"When you really want something, it is because that desire originated in the soul of the universe. It is your mission on earth."**

I remember the first time I heard those words. I was sitting at my desk as I was robotically inputting data into an excel file. The words called to me and jolted me out of my daze. My eyes began to well with tears. Yet, at the same time, my mouth curled into a smile. The words stabbed my heart like daggers and I felt a pain unlike anything before. When I pulled the daggers from my heart, I realized that no blood was drawn, but rather, something was given to me. The sharp teeth of the blades chewed away at the chains binding my heart to a destiny I did not desire. As I drew the daggers from the stone in my chest, sparks flew wildly and reignited a flame once lost.

Fire was Prometheus' gift to man. Since the dawn of time we have depended on the flame to warm us, to nourish us, and to light paths unseen.

I understood that I was given a second chance to wield my flame in hand and search for a new road. Although the destination of the path was not always clear to me, I decided to focus on the journey before me.

Every step I would take from that point on would be towards the real me, towards the future I dreamed of. A dream can never truly die. Although the blaze of ambition may fall silent, it only takes one spark and a breath of belief to make it roar.

For one year I planned. I wanted to begin pursuing my personal legend, like Santiago, in *The Alchemist*. I worked as many hours as I could, invested as much money as I could, and in one year I had saved up $7,500. I paid $5,000 of my hard-earned money so I could go searching for the name of the wind in the mountains of Spain. My college offered the opportunity to study Spanish abroad for one month at the University of Leon. The trip also included excursions on the weekends to Madrid, Basque Country, and Barcelona. I had also coordinated with some of the other students so that we could take a plane to Lisbon, Portugal for a weekend.

I can say with confidence that no one enjoyed that trip as much as me. Never in my life have I ever felt so free. I was disappointed to hear many people complain about the language barriers and some even said that the trip was a waste of their parent's money. On the other hand, I basked in the peace I felt in every second of my time there. I was thousands of miles away, but it was the first time in a while that I felt at home.

In the morning I would wake up an hour before class, so that I had some extra time to simply take in the beauty of Leon. I would grab my backpack, say goodbye to my host mom, and walk to the river. Once there I would sit under the shade of my favorite tree and start reading *For Whom the Bell Tolls* by Ernest Hemingway. I would get lost in those pages as I followed the tale of Robert Jordan as he fought in the Spanish Civil War. One scene in the book always stood out to me:

"He was completely integrated now and he took a good long look at everything. Then he looked up at the sky. There were big white clouds in it. He touched the palm of his hand against the pine needles where he lay and he touched the bark of the pine trunk that he lay behind."

This passage refers to Robert Jordan in his final moments. Throughout the course of the book, Robert did not understand the world of the abstract and the omens; his rational mind rejected such notions. However, in his final moments, he found peace in the world by letting go.

He accepted that he was going to die. He instructed his party to go on without him and escape, because he would only hinder them with his broken leg. As he said goodbye to the woman he fell in love with, Maria, he spoke of the abstract for the first time, "Although I must stay behind, I will be with you." He watched her leave with a stoic love in his heart and turned his head to the sky to say goodbye to the beautiful landscape of Spain that he had fallen in love with. As the fascists approached he aimed his pistol, barely conscious, and the story ends.

Even after finishing the book, I would open to that passage and fall evermore so in love with the landscapes that Robert Jordan adored enough to die for. I would sit there for an hour, allowing my thoughts to flow like the river beside me. The words, "fully integrated," have stayed with me for a long time. In my reflection, I would ask myself,

How often do I ignore the omens? What if I don't realize until the very end that life was speaking to me, like Robert? Paulo Coelho speaks of the omens and the soul of the universe as well. Have the omens brought me to Spain? Will King Melchizedek of Salem find me like Santiago? Will he provide me with Urim and Thummim to consult me on my journey? ... . Am I truly alive?

I have come to trust the signs that are presented to me in order to learn from Santiago and Robert. In Spain was the first time I truly heard the language of the omens and when they spoke to me, the words came as a challenge. They tested my will, but even in the face of critical situations, I put my faith in what was happening around me and remained steadfast while on my journey. When our class went to Pais Vasco (Basque Country), I lost my backpack at the beach. I had left it with my other classmates and I asked one of them to move my bag when they moved. However, they had forgotten. I was blissfully unaware of the ongoing situation as I swam about half a mile out to a platform that was floating in the distance. In that moment, my biggest concern came to me as I lay on my back floating. My head was beneath the water and all I could hear was the push and pull of the tide beneath me. Then suddenly, fear bubbled to the surface of my mind, "*What if a shark attacks me?!*"

I panicked for a moment, as I faced the possibility of living the fear I had thought so often about. I know it may seem irrational, but if I could rationalize my fear I wouldn't have it, now would I?! I think what scares me the most is not having control of the situation, or even the ability to see the attack coming. I am out of my element and grossly outclassed by my opponent. I could try to punch a shark in the gills, but I don't know if there is enough empirical data in the world to convince me to try and punch a shark in the face. The list of people that have punched a shark in the face is short, but those who did it and survived must be much shorter list. At least if I died after engaging in hand to tooth combat with a great white I would have a cool epithet: "Died after punching a shark in the face." When I finished calculating my statistical probability of survival and allowed my mind to settle, I took in the fact that I was swimming alone to this platform. However, I found resolution within myself. *"If a shark attacks me, so be it, I have found my peace. Maktub"*

After surviving a *potential* shark attack, a lost backpack was child's play. I told my friends that it had been misplaced and it had my valuables inside. You know, my phone, wallet, passport, aviators, and a necklace that is irreplaceable to me. These were *little things*. As expected, once one person started panicking, everyone started panicking. Someone thought it would be helpful to engage in a useless sequence of questioning with me: "Are you sure it's not here? Did you check where you last saw it? Did you look over there?" My irritation began to flare behind my eyes at how pointless those questions were. *"Obviously, I am sure it is not here, otherwise it would not be missing!"* I decided to walk away from the crowd, to clear my mind and retrace my steps. I went to the spot where I had originally laid my stuff, but it was consumed by the ocean. "Yeah! I'm pretty sure it's not here!" By a happy coincidence I spotted my t-shirt floating along the waves, so I knew that my stuff was there to say the least. I notice a couple speaking amongst themselves and looking at me, so

I decided to ask, in my very limited Spanish, "Me falta me mochilla, ustedes saben? *It really was more of a statement than a question and I was praying that they spoke Spanish.* In Pais Vasco most of the locals speak Castellano. Luckily, they seemed to know something about my backpack, so I called my friend over that spoke better Spanish than me. Apparently, these wonderful people turned my backpack into the lost and found. We sprinted towards the lost and found because my class was leaving the beach and preparing to board the bus. Upon arrival, I saw my backpack as well as another classmate's bag. The lady at the counter was kind. She opted to not charge me the 25 Euros to reclaim my items and sent me on my way. I opened my bag and with great relief I found that nothing was missing.

I had the biggest smile on my face as we ran towards the bus. When I regaled my concerned friends with the story of my luck, one of them spoke to me. "It's your karma Ethan. You have been nothing but kind to everyone on this trip. I can see it in you. The gratitude is written all over your face. This is why everything was returned to you." I paused to reflect on what she said. *"What an odd thing for her to say to me. I have never considered myself to be a lucky person, but this is crazy lucky. Just the other night someone lost their wallet and although it was returned, it was missing 200 Euros."* I smiled to her and said, "maybe you're right, maybe the omens are on my side."

The time I spent in Spain will always be near and dear to my heart. I have walked through the town of Segovia. I have swum at the beaches of Pais Vasco, Lisbon, and Barcelona. I have ventured through las cuevas and climbed las montañas de leon.

As I left Leon for the final time, I packed up my book and crossed the gently flowing river. I felt the uneven earth of the cobblestone road beneath my feet as I walked through the streets that I had become intimately acquainted with. I felt the breath of the wild swirl in my lungs with each inhale. For the first time in my life, I was able to let go of all the things that weighed me down. For the very first time,

I felt free.

I followed the omens and listened for the name of the wind. I became fully integrated with, the world.

Stargazing:

At the time, I had reached the end of a long relationship and I was prepared to be single for a little while. However, the omens do not care for arbitrary deadlines and designations; time is of the essence when they speak to you. A life changing opportunity may only exist for a moment. In this case, it felt like the omens were screaming at me to get my attention.

I would see her everywhere, even in my dreams. Every dose of her I had was never enough and still never is. Even from the first time I saw her, I felt that I knew her. I have always had the peculiar ability to spot a kindred soul, but when I looked into her eyes, I could see a piece of myself long since lost inside.

When we were still in the talking stages of the relationship, I had a dream about her that felt like a vision. Some of you may not believe the story when I tell it, but I have always dreamt astonishingly vividly.

Personally, I believe that it is a product of meditating:

I'm falling. . . falling again. . . I have had this dream so many times. Why am I always falling? I can feel the brush of the air wrapping around my body as I plummet towards the earth out of the

night sky. Suddenly my body crashes into the water and I begin to sink like I have so many times before. Air bubbles from the last bit of breath in my lungs fly towards the surface as I fall deeper into the depths. My eyelids grow heavy and the world is fading to black all over again. Right before my eyes close, I feel a push on my back and I rise towards the surface. On my back I look up at the stars in the sky unable to move. My body feels like it was magnetized to the ground. I watch as a star races out of the night sky and a streak of light lands on the water just 10 feet away from me. I struggle to move, but barely manage to lift my head. All I can manage to see are two bare feet standing on the water before me. The figure was a wearing a white dress and with each step she took towards me I regained more of my mobility. I crawled to her as we stood on the water's surface. The figure bent down and cupped a blue lotus flower in her hands. I raised my head to eye level and I saw her. Asvini. She is so beautiful; a crown of stars circled her head like a halo. Before I could finish saying her name, her cupped hands were at my chest. "How?" I said, confused and in disbelief. She smiled at me and said, "I believe this is yours." The flower passed through my chest and I could feel it in my heart. I said, "Thank you" and woke up.

I understand that this may seem like a tall tale to some of you, but to me, it was the most critical dream I have ever had. Upon waking up that morning, I knew that this was the girl I wanted to be with. Later that day, I told her my dream and what I had been feeling. Luckily for me, those feelings were returned in equal force. Oddly enough, she had been dreaming about me that night as well. We were both perplexed by the intensity of the emotions that we felt for one another. We were both fiercely independent people and were not the type to get attached too quickly.

Although we both said we wanted to take our time, loving her was the easiest thing I have ever done. I was completely enchanted; I was fully under her spell. Everything just flowed so naturally with her. We found ourselves talking about things we locked away for more than a decade. We showed each other who the other was behind the masks that we wore to protect our hearts. What I saw was the most beautiful person I have ever encountered in my life. Her true story inspired me; she had endured so much on her own for so long. She had to carry the brunt of struggles on her own, but she could always pull more strength from the well to keep pushing forward. Although she may have stumbled, she did it with such grace that it looked like dancing to me.

As it would turn out, among our many similarities, we both share a love for poetry. Admittedly, she is much better at writing poetry than me, to the point where I almost feel childish showing her mine. Despite that fact, she still inspires me to write. I wrote this poem for her when we first started dating:

Insomnia

by Ethan DeAbreu

Starlight climbs through my window
My mind drifts with the clouds
Lost in the midnight sky

The thought of your pores through
A smile curls my lips
A star dances in my soul

My heart is yours for you to keep
You are my dream so I need not sleep

Life is funny. It gives you many curves and turns in the road, which makes it all seem random Yet, somehow it still gets us to our destination. When I was a boy, I tried to seize the stars out of the sky. However, I was never successful. Today I stand as a man, with Asvini, the woman who is named after a constellation. *Finally, the stars were within my grasp.*

Chapter 7
ACTS OF REBELLION

Shrieking sirens scream. These sounds crawl along my bare skin leaving gooseflesh with each step. My eyes snap open, but I am lost and dazed . . . The fog of war can consume a man . . .

But I am no ordinary man and I will not relent. I shall not waver in the face of the enemy. My challenger meets my eyes with a smirk that was nearly luminescent in the night. I let the intensity pour out of me; I can feel the pressure of my presence fill the room.

I can feel my existence.

I slam my hand down and silence the enemy. His arrogant smirk fades into the darkness like it does every day. I take another glance at my phone, "4:07 AM." I suck my teeth and wince, "dammit, it took me seven minutes to win today."

Slowly, but surely, I leave the warmth of my bed. I close my eyes and let my body plummet towards the floor. I feel the sleeping air brush against my face and swirl in my ears. The moment of impact is imminent, no, it is inevitable. So what's next? Do I simply allow myself to fall? Or do I act? Perhaps some divine hand will swoop in and catch me before I meet the floor. However, I am not a betting man. I throw my hands forward and bury my palms into the earth.

I grunt, and then whisper to myself, "one-hundred."

With each repetition I bury that man. I push him beneath the floorboards and into the dirt. I killed him, simply because he was weaker than me. I despised the way he would whine and complain when faced with adversity. For seven minutes, he ruled my mind. For seven minutes, I was ready to take a day off. I was willing to walk away from all my dreams. It was as the Japanese adage goes:

"Fall down seven times, stand up eight"

"七転び八起き"

Oh, the enemy can be quite persuasive. He greets me as a friend and pretends to have my best interests at heart. His gentle voice guides me towards the warmth of my bed. "You worked hard yesterday, so it's okay to rest today. You need your rest if you want to change the world. Maybe you will even reach your dreams as you drift away on the clouds." He'll tell me that it is okay to sleep in today because it's too cold outside and I might freeze if I leave. He'll tell me that it is raining outside and I could get sick if I go for a run. My eyelids slowly retreat into slumber, but then hear another voice, "is that it?"

The real threat we face every day is complacency. Remaining the same takes no effort at all, but it costs us more than anything. As human beings we are malleable; we are never a finished project. Each day we have the responsibility to hammer the metal of our mind. With each strike of the hammer sparks fly. We refine ourselves; we reinforce our greater selves.

I am both the steel of my mind and the hammer that strikes it.

Luckily, for the past five years now, that other voice makes itself heard. My voice of strength does not always get through to me. I would be lying to you if I pretended that it did. I am human after all, and there are some days when we are simply burnt out. However, on the days when I do go back to sleep, I always regret it. On the other hand, I have never regretted a workout.

I started getting up at 5 am as a freshman in college. One evening my mom came up to me and mentioned an article she had read about how the most successful people in the world get up at 5 am. The thought stirred in my mind for a little bit. I have always been success driven and the idea of being part of a club that grouped me in with my heroes inspired me. The very next morning, my alarm sounded at 5:00 am and I immediately hit snooze and went back to sleep like a "normal person." Later in the day, I found myself reflecting on my decision to hit snooze and grimaced when the feeling of shame spilt over me. I felt ashamed because I had not even tried to change. I just went right back to what I knew. The word "normal" was echoing in the chambers of my mind. I hated the word, the idea, of being *normal*. I would try again tomorrow morning. No matter how tired I was, I was going to move.

The time came once again and this time I rose without hesitation. I didn't check my phone. I didn't go on Facebook or check my Instagram. I got out of bed and got dressed. Without a doubt I was groggy, and yeah, it was cold. However, with one foot in front of the other, I walked out the front door. With each step, I eased into my rhythm, I started taking longer strides and each time I planted my foot into the ground, I found myself enjoying the experience a little more. Was I enjoying running in the freezing cold as the frigid November air stabbed my lungs? No. . . I'm not a masochist.

I was enjoying the challenge; I was proud of myself for making the difficult decision. I was smiling because that was the moment I officially joined the 5 am club: the minority of the world. After my run, I came home, showered, and began studying before driving to college.

My mom came out of her room and to her surprise, she found that the coffee was already started and I was on my second cup. Yeah, I used pumpkin creamer. JUDGE ME. With her puzzled look, she asked, "What are you doing up?" She said it how she always says it. Her eyes narrowed, face scrunches up, and the words leave her lips faster than she thinks of them. It's little moments like these that I will always treasure. Whenever she asked me that question I was always in the middle of a new experiment or transition. Although her question was always "what" I would answer with my "why." I just smiled and said, "I did it." She smiled back, and went for a cup of coffee herself. When you are truly close to someone, you don't need words to communicate; you can just stare in the windows of the soul and see what is written on the glass.

Unfortunately, the next semester demanded that I be on campus by 7:15 am for my classes. Throughout my college career, I drove 50 miles one way to school and balanced working 25 to 40 hours a week. It appeared that I would no longer be able to participate in the 5 am club and I found it disheartening. I learned to love my morning routine and I was reluctant to give it up. In that moment, I asked myself, "What if I pushed my body to get up another hour earlier?" Then I decided, if I can't have my 5 am routine, I will have my 4am one. I had already pushed my limits once, so doing it again should be familiar territory.

We are perpetually battling the demands the world places on us, but rarely demand more from ourselves. There was no room for negotiation; I wasn't going to drop the hammer and accept the product as is. I was in the middle of "the process."

No, I am still in the middle of the process, even as you read. I am still striking the hammer and refining the blade of my mind. We have to learn how to ask more of ourselves and respond to the demands that our dreams and goals place on us. Change is difficult to achieve overnight. In some cases, it may even take two!

The reason why many people fail to achieve meaningful change is because they are relying on motivation instead of discipline. Simply put, if you rely on motivation to achieve your goals, you will never reach them.

Why Motivation Just Isn't Good Enough:

If you wait to be motivated to begin working on your dreams, you will only know the poverty of unrealized potential. Motivation is far too temperamental to be used to fuel your ambition. Sure, it feels great to be motivated, but that chemical reaction has a very short half-life.

In your inspired state, you burn all of your energy in a brilliant blaze of flame, but you don't feel the way you expected. Although the flames of your ambition burnt white hot just moments before, they are now extinguished. Simply put, you're exhausted. You didn't accomplish nearly as much work as you had anticipated and you are not too sure about doing this again tomorrow.

I have seen this happen countless times and of course, I too have been drawn to the allure of motivation. Motivation is like a nuclear reactor. It is a powerhouse of energy, but not necessarily the best place to get it. If you had the choice of using a nuclear reactor or a stream of water to power your home, which would you use? Assuming you're not a fan of yellow cake and glowing in the dark, you would probably choose the latter. In order to harness hydroelectricity, you may need to build a dam. Building the dam will certainly take time, but in the long term, relying on steadily flowing water rather than unstable elemental composites will leave you in a more favorable position. You can be active instead of *radioactive (I know I am terrible for that one).*

Some may argue that nuclear energy generates more energy, but I am not the "live fast die young" sort of guy. I am building the infrastructure in my mind in order to consistently pull energy for the rest of my life.

> ***If you are not achieving the goal you set after, then you are simply not working hard enough.***

That being said, how can you work hard without burning out? If motivation isn't enough, what can you do?

You Must Discipline Your Mind:

If you begin a marathon with a sprinter mentality, you will find yourself gassed after the first 400 meters. Motivation fails you as a fuel source because it is just a momentary burst of energy; it burns far too quickly to be sustained.

Motivation is unreliable because it is reliant upon your feelings, whereas discipline is a philosophy. There will absolutely be mornings when you just feel like garbage. Days where you don't feel a drop of energy in the tank to get you out of bed.

Honestly, there are some days when I get out of bed that I am so tired that it feels like I'm drunk. Or if it's a Wednesday, hungover. Despite that awful feeling and the gravity of the exhaustion that tethers me to the ground, I move. I stumble into the kitchen and make my workout drinks. I down my pre-workout and I'm out the door with BCAAs and a Whey protein shake. Eventually, I feel the tingly sensation of the beta-alanine coursing through me as I blast 'Pull the Trigger by Russ' in my car. I'm waking up. I am getting in the zone as I listen to the words, "Pull the trigger, ain't nobody gonna do it for you. Don't hesitate, just shoot." I am remembering "why" I set the alarm. Absolutely no one will be, or should be, more invested in your dreams than you. If you want to achieve something, it is entirely on your shoulders to make the decisions that take you there. Do you think your friends will care if you tell them, "yeah, I was too tired to work out today?" No, they couldn't care less. They will just accept whatever you say as trivial complaining and move on with their day.

Although it may not bother your friends when you don't work on your dreams, it should bother you. You should hear the nagging voice of guilt that keeps asking you, "why didn't you do it?" Stop making excuses as to why you didn't have enough time to work towards the life you dream of.

Every morning, I make the choice to work on my happiness, the happiness of my family, and eventually maybe even yours. The rationale I have given myself is this, "You can't free the world unless you can free yourself. You can't empower others with your words, if you cannot find strength in them yourself." Every morning when I wake up, I like to think that everyone is depending on me to free myself. So when I feel weak and groggy, I pull my strength from the well of the people. I ask myself, "You wanted to change the world, didn't you? Did you think it would be easy?"

The philosophy of discipline is rooted in accountability. The terrifying truth of the world is that we are in control of our lives. If we are unhappy, it is because that we made the decisions that took us there. By that logic, we must be able to make the decisions necessary to achieve happiness in life. The problem is that no one takes responsibility for their circumstances. These people always have the same colorless excuses:

> "Well if it weren't for this, then I'd be that"
> "With the hours I work there is just no time"
> "How do I pay the bills and build my dreams?"
> "I just don't have the energy"
> If you find yourself saying even one of these things, it is likely you are unhappy.
> People that work towards achieving their dreams say things like:
> "I started reading this new book!"
> "I have this interesting idea I want to test out."
> "I have a new goal and this is how I am going to reach it."

> "Sleep? I wish I didn't need it so I can
> keep working on my goals."

Okay, maybe the last one is a bit of a reach for some people. However, I genuinely wish I didn't need to sleep for the sake of productivity. Think about how ridiculous it is that your body just shuts down for hours on end. However, I digress.

Where does strength come from?

Strength is born from **discipline**; it is born from absolute mental fortitude. Discipline comes from having an unshakable resolve to achieve your goals. When you make the realization of your ambition your top priority, everything else is just white noise. Discipline is a renewable source of energy because it exists in your mind; it is the power of choice. Greatness is a choice, you either take the actions to earn it or you don't.

The moment your alarm rings, jump out of bed. If you hesitate, you lose. There has to be conviction in your words, thoughts, and actions. You set that alarm for a reason, so act upon it. Change is never an easy process. However, in time, you find a rhythm to what you are doing. Although the work is trying, it is rewarding. If you make the necessary sacrifices, you will reap the benefits.

The best way to apply discipline in your life is to simply pause and ask yourself "why." Reflect on what you are doing at the current moment, then apply it to your goals. If what you are currently doing cannot benefit you in the long run, then you can better delegate your time. You must hold yourself accountable for your own success. It is a brutal, and at times, lonely road, but it is your choice to walk it. Honestly, pause right now, and ask yourself, "what do I want?"

You have to be willing to face the questions that can throw you into an existential crisis. Chaos is better than complacency. One needs to feed the chaos within and then command it. We can only grow if we challenge ourselves to exceed our limitations. Reach into your soul and gather the pieces of your dreams. Then, start taking actions towards it. If you are perpetually hitting the snooze on your alarm, you will never even come close to your dreams.

Start today, go after all that you are worth.

When I day dream:

I often find myself lost in thought. Many times, I think of my heroes. These are people that have changed the world:

Tony Robbins, Arnold Schwarzenegger, Muhammad Ali, Bruce Lee, Paulo Coelho, Tim Ferris, Gary Vayneerchuck, and Scott Harrison.

They inspire me, so maybe hearing a little about them will inspire you too?

Tony Robbins: He donated all the profits from his book MONEY Master the Game, along with a personal contribution, to donate 57 million meals to the Non-Profit, "Feeding America." His donation was part of an even bigger plan to inspire the public to match his donations in order to reach 100 million meals.

Arnold Schwarzenegger: He left his home in Austria and came to The United States to begin his quest to become "the greatest bodybuilder in history." He won the title of Mr. Universe at age 20 and as the years went on, he achieved the title of Mr. Olympia seven times. He was always working towards the next thing on his list of goal, and never took "no" for an answer. His mindset and work ethic lead him to Hollywood Stardom; he even became the "Governator" of California.

Muhammad Ali: A true icon of American History. He was more than just a boxing champion; he was the champion of the people. His charisma and passion played an important role inspiring people in the battle for equality in America. I can't do him justice in a paragraph, but when I think of him, I can understand why people loved him.

Bruce Lee: I was first thrilled by watching him perform in the movies. However, as time went on, he became my first well of strength. Bruce Lee was my first real hero. He inspired me because he was constantly pushing his body to redefine the line between myth and reality. I respected him as a martial artist and philosopher. He said that, "In life there are no limits, only plateaus."

Paulo Coelho: He wrote the book that changed my life, The Alchemist. This book came to me at the right time and it pushed me to ask the question, "Do I really believe in myself?" It also contained the words that inspired me to take a chance on love and my heart has never felt so full.

Tim Ferris: He has provided me with so much learning and value in the last three years. He wrote the iconic *Four Hour Work Week* and is the host of both *FearLess* and *The Tim Ferris Show* podcasts. As I sat at my desk at work, or drove hours on end in the car, his interviews inspired me to keep pushing. I would often tease myself and say, "if you work hard enough, maybe he would want to interview you. You will then have a chance to sit with one of your heroes."

Gary Vayneerchuck: The dark horse of the world of motivation. Above all other things, I respect his forwardness. He prides himself on achieving the American dream after he immigrated with his family to the United States from Soviet Russia. He would probably tattoo the word "hustle" on the forehead of his first born; however, he doesn't need to, his work ethic says it all. He is brutally honest and puts all goals in their simplest terms: "What is it? How do I achieve it? Hustle."

Scott Harrison: Created a Non-Profit that works towards giving millions of people clean drinking water. This is something we take for granted almost every day. He invests 100% of the donations acquired to build an infrastructure in developing countries that can provide people with readily available drinking water. Water is the essence of life. While we take our 40-minute showers and drink our eight glasses of it a day, others have to walk for four hours to get some. In most cases, the water they acquire festers diarrheal diseases that claim the lives of millions each year. His mission won't be over until, "Nobody dies from unclean drinking water."

When I think about those great people, I think about how they came to their achievements. Every single one of them is a self-made legend. They didn't get placed on the "fast path to success." They achieved their goals through grit, tenacity, and devotion to their mission. While the rest of the world slept, they were working. Hard work is not a gift, you don't have to be special to work hard. You don't have to be rich or good looking. You just have to pay your dues, every day, every hour, and every second. Bills are expensive, but ignoring your dreams is true poverty.

One day, long from now, I want my words and my actions to be what inspired someone who felt defeated to keep going. I want to be the voice you hear when you are debating going to the gym. I want to be the one that is there for you when you are debating taking an opportunity to be charitable. I want to be the one to prevent you from giving up on your dreams. My discipline is rooted in the belief that I, as human being, have the power to change the world by touching the hearts of all people with my actions and words.

Chapter 8
SMALL ACTS OF KINDNESS

I often contemplate, "What is the value of a life, and what is the value in mine?"

Can the value of a life be measured in terms of hours, minutes, and seconds? Perhaps the value of a life is literal and can be appraised by the things we own.

Every day we are faced with the task of understanding the meaning of our existence. More often than not, it is far too daunting of an objective for us to truly bring ourselves to face. We are perpetually choosing between the ultimatum of walking towards the person we are meant to be and walking away. For many people, it is more like running away from the person they are meant to be. However, if you spend your life running, you will reach an assured destination of existential crisis. Your frenzied sprint fueled by fear will leave you lost and exhausted. This all happens whilst you ask yourself the one cumbersome question, "where did I make a wrong turn?"

I find myself asking that question quite a bit. Both because of existential crisis and my conventionally terrible sense of direction. Although I don't always know where I am going, I try not to panic when I get lost. I try to think of it more as the scenic route towards my destination. In my heart, I have always felt that the destination ahead of me is inevitable, so I might as well learn to love the walk. On a side note, while on my first date with Asvini in the city, I told her "I promise you two things: First, we are absolutely going to get lost. Second, today will be the best date you ever had."

August 3rd, 2017

On an ordinary Thursday afternoon, I took an impromptu adventure into the city with a good friend of mine. We are both amateur photographers. We may not have millions of followers, but we are genuine. We walk out into the world with our cameras in hand, hoping to see something beautiful so that we may share it with others.

I began thinking of something another friend of mine said, a long while ago. He quoted Einstein and said to me,

"There are two ways you can live your life: one is as though nothing is a miracle. The other is as though everything is a miracle."

In an instant, I press down on the black, rounded trigger. I hear the shot being fired. The black curtain rapidly pulls away and light floods the stage. The show has begun and it has ended. However, in that moment of clarity, I think I may have understood what he meant.

My inner contemplation faded away as I bore witness to something that tore into the fibers of my heart.

As I walked along the sidewalk on this sunny summer day, I saw an older man lying with his back to the wall. His feet were bare, his clothes torn, and his face was masked with a thick salt and pepper beard. He was crying for help, shouting at people in frustration and in disbelief, "I don't understand why you can't help! I am hungry, and thirsty! Please . . . someone . . . anyone . . . can't anyone help. . ."

The heart of the empath is susceptible to flooding. I was drowning in a sea of emotions. First, I felt immense sadness because the desperation in his voice echoed in my bones. Then a white-hot anger filled me, "how can people be so cruel, he is a human being. He has the right to live!" In the end, my heart whispered to me, "be the first to help and perhaps others will see." I patted my friend on the shoulder and gave him a knowing look. I said to him, "I have to."

I approached the disheartened man and introduced myself. He introduced himself as "Geezus." He explained that his name was like Jesus, but with a "G". I asked him, "is there something I could get you to eat?"

His eyes began to flood with tears, so he quickly jerked his head to side so I would not notice. With a tightly coiled body he said, "I would be very happy with a cheeseburger and a coke." I was happy to oblige. I walked over to the nearest food cart and ordered just that. The owner asked me, "is it for him?" I could see that he was genuinely surprised, but not quite sure how he felt about it. I spoke to him with sincerity in my voice and said, "it is for the brother I never knew." I looked at the $20 bill in my wallet and handed it to the man with a smile and said, "until the next time, thank you."

I walked over to Geezus and gave him the lunch he requested and noticed that he was deep in conversation with my friend. His whole demeanor had changed in the time it took for me to walk away and walk back. His shoulders relaxed and his arm rested on one knee as he leaned forward in conversation. Most importantly there was a smile on his face and light in his eyes. He thanked me for the meal and wished us well. Before we left, my friend took his portrait and some days I look at it and wonder how he is doing.

We went along with our day and the thought occurred to me, "what if I dedicated the remaining $13 in my wallet to helping others?"

Later, I gave $5 to a Buddhist monk that was trying to build a temple. He gave me a bracelet that was jade green and said a prayer as he put it on my wrist. I gave him a smile, wished him well, and continued down my path.

I then placed $3 in the cup of a man that was sleeping, followed by another $4 to a woman that said she was pregnant.

As for the last dollar, I simply dropped into the street. I watched from the corner of my eye as the bill was carried away with the flow of the crowd. Perhaps, someone who was feeling a little down on their luck would find it and it would brighten their day.

Although I went into the city that day to find something beautiful, I came to realize that the greatest beauty we can experience is in giving to others. Perhaps I am simply young and naive, but I believe that small acts of kindness can change the world. As for the matter of "when" will the world change, well, that is entirely up to *you*.

Kindness does not have to be elaborate or grandiose. You don't need a lot of money and you don't need a lot of time. The only things you need to be kind are to learn how to give without wanting anything in return and learn how to smile with your soul.

Behind our eyes, which are the windows to the soul, we hide our true selves. While some hide like snakes in the grass, others hide like a scared child. The pain we have experienced can become our prison, or it can be the key to connecting with another lost soul. We lock ourselves away from the world in order to protect ourselves from suffering. Although we may feel safe behind our four walls, *are we truly free?*

We all suffer from the human condition. We starve for connection, but fear pain and rejection. However, to fear pain is to fear life. In our suffering we find our humanity. We become humbled and we learn how to give the love we needed to others. Don't be afraid of life; embrace it for all the good and the bad. Although we will endure pain outside of our mental walls, at least we are free.

March 3rd, 2012: Kindness That Touched My Soul

For the first time in many years, I allowed myself to cry. My tears flowed neither from pain or anger, but gratitude.

At the time I had been preparing tirelessly for a competition. I was a "lawyer" for the NYS Youth and Government Club and in the following week I would be going upstate to debate. This year was going to be different from last year. I had suffered a heart crushing defeat last year. My team was systematically destroyed from the inside out. Last year, after months of preparation, our team was ready; however, a teammate of mine had feigned having laryngitis in order to excuse herself from competing at the last moment. In reality she was not ill; she simply was unprepared to debate and it was far too late for my other teammate and myself to learn her parts. We went into the courtroom and plead our case. Unfortunately, our unprepared teammate, the one who feigned illness, suddenly decided to participate. When she talked, her argument was in favor of the opposing side. The next day we endured the embarrassment of hearing how we lost in excruciating detail. I am not a sore loser. I often seek challenges where I am at a disadvantage because the thrill of combating insurmountable odds excites me. However, this defeat was different. I felt that the loss occurred not because I was outclassed by my opponent, but rather that my teammate did not share our commitment for victory. This defeat lit a fire in me and I was determined to come back next year and seize the reigns of victory. I would not let it slip out of my grasp due to lack of tenacity.

Unbeknownst to my mother, I had been walking 5 miles alone, at night, for months, in order to get to the club meetings. My mom worked very late nights and wasn't home to take me to the meetings in time. I hated relying on other people to get me to the club because on one occasion a parent openly expressed her irritation to me about having to pick me up. I decided that I would just walk alone in order to spare myself from enduring that sort of humiliation again. The circumstances didn't matter. Rain, snow, or freezing temperatures did not deter me; I was on a mission. As the cold air stabbed at my lungs, my fire raged to keep me warm. With each step my mantra was, "I am walking the path to victory." I had to embrace a mentality that was absolute; my walking was not in vain because my victory was inevitable.

My competition was one week away and this year I didn't have to worry about hotel or the travel costs because I fundraised the full $175 by selling cookie dough to teachers. The only thing left to do was put on my suit and go. However, as I went to try on my suits from the previous year, I encountered a critical problem. Although I had gotten leaner in the past year from working out, I had become more broad-shouldered. In short, I didn't fit into my suit. My mom began to panic a bit because money was tight. I felt so guilty that I put her in this position that I suggested that it wasn't a big deal and that I could just go next year. At a young age I understood the stress on my mother's shoulders and how hard she had to work to provide for us. As such, I worked incessantly and independently so that she would not have to worry about me, yet here I was. I was prepared to let go because I felt it was my duty to her.

My small family has had a motto that has kept us going in the direst of circumstance, "Just figure it out somehow." My mother had shared my circumstances with her boyfriend at the time, Chris. He told her not to worry and that he would get me everything I needed for the competition. At first, I didn't believe him. Many people have promised to help me, but it always fell through. So, I didn't think much of it. I have never been the type of person that allowed himself to get his hopes up, because it seemed like every time I did, they were crushed.

On Sunday morning, he knocked at my door and said, "go get dressed young man, we have some suits to buy today." In disbelief, I got dressed and before I knew it, I was at the Men's Warehouse with him. When I looked at the prices of the suits, my heart dropped and the doubt crept into my mind again, *"it's so expensive, there is no way he is going to spend that much money on me..."* I felt so ashamed and embarrassed. I told him, "everything here is really expensive. You don't have to do this for me, I understand."

"Young man, I told you already that we are here to buy you suits, so you can kick some butt upstate" he said.

He began picking out shirts and asking me if I liked them. Of course, I did, but none of them were on sale . . .

"He is going to pay full price . . .for me?" I thought to myself.

When I woke up from my trance of disbelief I was being fitted for a suit. *My suit.* Chris said, with great enthusiasm, "you look very sharp, *very sharp!*"

I smiled and started to allow myself to let my guard down, but as we walked to the register, all the stress I had forgotten a moment ago came rushing back.

"$767.34"

My heart dropped and I felt my tears welling up in my eyes, "It's okay Chris, really, I don't need them." He smiled at me, "Don't be silly, I am happy to do it."

As we exited the store, I was the very proud owner of three pairs of dress pants, three dress shirts, three ties, and one suit jacket. I walked a few paces ahead of him to hide my tears. Someone who I wasn't even related to did all of this for me.

We went to the pizzeria to grab a slice and I sat there. I was unsure how I could ever pay him back. I walked to the register and bought two Italian ices. I gave him one and said, "I know it's not much, but from the bottom of my heart, thank you."

When I went home, I tried on my suits and looked at myself in the mirror. Almost immediately, I started crying uncontrollably. Then I started laughing. I was so grateful that my mom found a way to get me the suits I needed. For one of the first times in my life, a man stood up to help me. I walked up to the mirror one more time, my eyes red from the salt in my tears, and said, "I am going to win."

The next week flew by and it was now time to get on the bus so we could drive to the capitol for the next six hours. Right before I boarded, my mother smiled and handed me a gift, "It's a good luck present, I'm proud of you."

She bought me the pair of Ray-ban Aviators I wanted. They had green lenses and gold temples. My eyes began to well up with tears again. I gave my mom a hug and said, "Thank you, I'm going to win."

I went up to Albany, assured of my inevitable success, because so many people believed in me. In 2012, I was awarded the title of "Best Attorney in NYS." I also won the honors of, "Best Law firm" and "Judicial Exemplar." I have never been prouder. Victory begins when you first envision it in your mind. Without the support of my family, I would have never had the opportunity to test my mettle and redeem myself. That memory has always served as a testament to the power of our family motto. Even when the odds are against us, and defeat seems inevitable, we will always find a way.

Hands Stained Black:

My friend Bobby had arrived at my house at the normal 8:10 am so that we could catch our 8:40 train to Penn Station. Unfortunately, the Ronkonkoma line had been shut down for maintenance, so we had to depart from Babylon. The morning was rather gloomy. Grey clouds masked the sun and the scent of fresh rain was abundant. We arrived at Babylon Station about 15 minutes early and we began to feel nostalgic. In freshman year of college, we didn't have our licenses so we would spend about 5 hours a day commuting on the train to school. We both hadn't taken the Babylon line since we received our licenses nearly three years ago. It was just oddly satisfying to see how far we had come in just three years. It felt like the classic story line of the hero returning to his roots.

Our trip down memory lane was interrupted by the announcement of the conductor that our train was on track 2. We boarded and slowly gathered our friends with each passing stop. We arrived promptly at 10:34 and fed our New Yorker instincts with toasted everything bagels. We then ventured to Battery Park. My initial cynicism deduced that the name was derived from assault and battery. However, I was incorrect. The term "battery" was applied in reference to the battery of cannons that had once protected the port. At this point it seemed the skies had begun to clear, as if the cannons were piercing holes in the waves of grey.

Later, we walked to Frauces Tavern. I knew that this building was our next stop because it was the only Federal style building on the block. Dr. Russo paused, and I knew the question he was going to ask, so I just said "Federal." He was surprised that I was able to guess what he was about ask, and exclaimed "no way!"

He was my first professor when I came to Molloy and somehow it seemed fitting that he would be one of the last. It's funny how things tend to come full circle.

The tavern was interesting to say the least. It seemed like a great spot to just sit down and have some bacon and eggs off of a hot iron skillet. Dismissing my hunger impulses, I listened to the tour guide. She explained that George Washington had done a lot of his planning during the Revolutionary War here. Frauces Tavern was essentially where the Versailles of the Revolutionary War was held. Although the exhibits were of simple things, I could appreciate that this building was a small piece of history that didn't exactly make the textbooks.

Our day of history brought us to perhaps the most sacred and hallowed grounds in all of New York City. I could feel the raw emotions that were charging the air around us. I started walking slowly towards the infinity pool. I put my hands on the monument and just reflected on what had once stood there. The memorial consists of two one-acre pools set in the footprints of the original twin towers. My mind began to drift towards the day of the attack. I remembered my mom taking my brother and I out of school. I remember the panicked look on her face. Her eyes were wide and muscles were tense. I was quite pleased to be out of school early, until I saw her face. I asked her, as children do, what was wrong? She was unable to answer me. What could she say? She simply said that she would explain once we got back home. We were not allowed to watch T.V. when we got home, but my mind was too curious. I ended up turning on the T.V. and watched with confusion as I witnessed a plane crash into the Twin Towers. My mom called my brother and I into her room and explained using her makeup what had happened to the buildings. She was panicked because she had believed that my father's building may have been destroyed in the attacks. I began to feel the anxiety in my chest. I understood that my father may have been in danger and it frightened me. I spent the day in my room. I was scared and confused. Children have no wars, but it seemed that men thrived on it. I couldn't understand what would make someone want to hurt people like that. This type of thought was beyond my years... Luckily enough, it turned out my father was actually in Connecticut that day on business. My reflection was interrupted as a man began to enter my personal space. He was meticulously rubbing his hands across the names engraved. Moving from side to side with great care, the man wanted to cover every inch of the monument.

Immediately, I was interested in what he was doing. I watched for another minute before I gathered enough courage to ask him "why, are you doing that?" I tried to sound as friendly as possible to convey a genuine interest. His immediate response was, "because they are dusty." I knew there was more to the story, so I asked, "how does seeing the monument in this state make you feel." From there he decided to share with me his true heart and a beautiful story.

He explained that he is a firefighter and that this was his first time at the monument. He was only eleven when the attacks occurred and he said that he didn't know that he would ultimately become a firefighter. He said that looking at the monument made him reflect on the feelings of his brothers before him, "they could have never anticipated facing something on this scale."

His name was Dustin. He told me that he had spent the last hour scrubbing the names engraved to honor them. It had upset him that they were dusty. He told me that they deserved a lot more respect than that. I saw that he was anxious to return to his mission, so I shook his hand that was stained black and wished him well.

I am glad that my curiosity outweighed my hesitation. There are many delightful stories hidden in the world and sometimes a simple "why" may reveal them.

To all those who wonder how they can change the world, start with small acts of kindness. A single act of kindness is like throwing a pebble into the ocean. Although you may feel cynical about the extent of your impact when compared to the vastness of the ocean, you must remember that the ocean and all the waves and ripples we make in it are one and the same. Waves do not exist independently of the ocean; the ripples we make can be felt throughout the world.

Never doubt the impact you can leave on the world. Your potential to become a force for good is as vast as all the great oceans of the world. Alone we are powerful, but together, we are unstoppable.

Chapter 9
FORGIVENESS

It's 4:00 am again and my alarm has sounded calling me to battle. I stumbled into the kitchen half awake and trifled through the cabinets for my supplements. I mixed my preworkout with some orange juice, grimaced as I gulped it down, grabbed my bags, and I was out the door. It was rather brisk for September, but I paid it no mind as I made my way to the gym. It was only when the clerk at the counter greeted me did I fall out of my routine, "Good morning. . . Oh! And happy birthday!"

I paused in confusion. It slowly dawned on me that it was indeed my birthday again. Yet another year had come and gone. I had been working so much that I nearly forgot my own birthday. Luckily for the past four years, the clerk at the counter had been the first person to wish me. He was the one to bring me back to reality.

"Wow . . .has it really been four years?" I thought to myself in my groggy, decaffeinated state.

As I hit the weights, I found myself lost in reflection, "four years ago I was a senior in high school and now I am about to graduate college." These last few weeks have been grueling between work, school, and my personal life. Now that I think about it, I don't even have time to celebrate today. At the end of my workout I will be off to Melville, so I can sit behind my desk for a few hours. After work I will be driving to school for yet another exciting opportunity to sit behind a desk for a few hours. All in all, today is just another day that I have to power through. I won't even be home until 10:30 pm tonight.

As the day went on, I enjoyed some niceties and good wishes here and there. However, I was on autopilot. The day was passing me by. My lips would move to speak to people, yet there was no conscious thought behind it. Before I knew it, it was 6:45 in the evening and I was sitting in my Cost Accounting class. I didn't hate or love this class.

I just knew I wasn't thrilled to have to sit there for the next three hours. At least night classes aren't so bad. If you pay attention for more than 15 minutes you are bound to score in the upper quartile of the class. My eyes felt swollen and heavy from the exhaustion of the day. I opened up my laptop and began preparing my notes for class. With my earphones in, I found myself thinking, "welcome to 21, where every day just looks the same." My small bout of cynicism was interrupted by a figure standing in front of me. An old friend hovered above me, her eyes were bright and her smile was even brighter. She abruptly said, "Surprise!" As she presented me with a white paper bag. The bag had a picture of the two of us, with another friend of ours from our times in Spain and Portugal. The sentiment pulled at my heartstrings. When I opened it up, I found that it had a can of Sumol in it and a dessert called "nata". These were two of my favorite things. Sumol is a popular Portuguese orange flavored carbonated juice. When I found it in Lisbon, my friends saw how excited

I was and they must have remembered. Nata in its immediate translation is "cream", but it deserves so much more than that. It is absolutely heavenly. Its crisp crust has the most satisfying crunch. In that first big bite you taste luscious custard cream that is lightly torched at the top with caramelized sugar. *If you couldn't tell, I have a thing for food.* A big smile crawled onto my face and I felt some of the exhaustion leave me. What a lovely and warm gesture for a brisk September day.

Before I knew it, I was walking into my house again. As I went into the kitchen, I saw that the time was 10:47 pm. There was some traffic on the way home, because on Long Island, it doesn't matter what time you leave, there is always traffic. On the kitchen counter, I saw a six pack of beer on the table with my name on it and a pile of birthday cards. I smiled to myself and I was grateful to have a mom that can make me smile even when she was asleep.

As I went through the cards, I saw one that had handwriting that I knew all too well. My eyes narrowed and my gentle smile was curved into a smirk. It was a card from my father. This may seem ordinary to most people, but at the time it had been five years since I last spoke a word to him. When I opened his card, I was surprised to find a letter and a check. Usually I just get a generic card with nothing inside that is signed in a "matter of fact way" at the bottom, "Love, *your Father.*"

"Hmm, 'Father' now that is a word I have tried to escape for a long time" I thought. It's hard to run away when you even have the same name. My first name has always served as a bitter reminder that he indeed was my father and that regardless of what I do, we were bound together in blood and in name.

Although we may share the same blood type and the same first name, my real name is "Ethan" and no one can take that away from me. There have been so many times when I seriously considered changing my first name and my last name. I still consider it, *"why do others get to choose my identity?"* I just wanted to start fresh, without any connections to names that try to own and define me.

I took a breath and began reading his letter. It was difficult for me to chew through his words, but then I thought about how difficult it was for him to write it. My father was never the type to express his emotions. He was always the disciplinarian: militant and straightforward. I was reading the reflection of a tired and sad man. He tried to explain that he loved us in his own way, "To raise and support a family you need money, love is what got me up in the morning to go to work to make that money to support my family." I understand his mentality and where it came from. My grandfather, his father, immigrated to the United States from Guyana with $17 in his pocket. He left Guyana, where he was relatively wealthy, in order to create a better life for his three children. My grandfather worked for pennies an hour in a sweatshop. He tirelessly carried on in order to plant the seeds for a better future. Over many years, he climbed through the ranks, running on less than 4 hours of sleep a night in order to create his American Dream. Naturally, with him working all the time, my father as the eldest sibling had to take on more responsibility than a normal child would. *Just like me.* His image of what a man is came from watching my grandfather. To him, a man is a "provider."

My father carried a heavy burden on his shoulders throughout his childhood and eventually joined the Marine

Corps. If I were to score my father on the Myers Briggs Personality test, I imagine that he would score ISTJ, (Introvert, Sensing, Thinking, and Judging). His personality type, coupled with a military attitude, created a creature of cold rationality. He is without a doubt one of the most intelligent people I have ever encountered. However, my father has a mind that operates like an excel spreadsheet, just "if then" statements there is no in-between. On the other hand, I score as an "INTJ" (Introvert, Intuitive, Thinking, Judging). Without a doubt, I am a creature of logic like my father, but, the critical difference is that I have a stronger foundation of empathy. I was never satisfied with "if then." I wanted to know the "why" and the "how." While I'm at it, my mother is certainly an INFJ (Introverted, Intuitive, Feeling, and Judging). I have found myself in between their two personalities, teetering on the edge of rationality and empathy.

Although, I can understand his rationale. He felt his job was to be the provider. However, parenting is much more than providing. You did support my family and I thank you for that. However, you didn't want to be a part of the family. Things were not so black and white as simply saying that you "did your best to provide for us." Although it is a difficult reality to face, it is true. There were many things that you did that hurt my family for years to come. When you left it broke all of our hearts, not just my mother's.

A child idolizes his parents and wants them to be perfect. Now I understand that no one is perfect; everyone is just trying to do their best. The reason why you became the most hated person in my life is because *I loved you the most.* You were my hero. I wanted to grow up to be as smart and strong as you; I believed that you could do anything. We all want our heroes to acknowledge us. However, the words that you shared with me always beat me down. You used your powers to take rather than give. You took every ounce of love out of my heart. I worked so hard to prove you wrong; I wanted to show you that I could fly too because I was your son. *Sadly, you tore my paper wings.*

In your letter you wished me, "Happiness, maturity, wisdom, and love." I spent a great deal of time thinking about your words. I spoke about my surprise with mom. As always, she encouraged me to talk to you and regaled me with stories about how we were impossible to separate when I was young. However, that was then and this is now. You seem to think that I abandoned you, but, when you really think about it, "who left first?"

You even took Sabrina, our dog, away from us. She was not yours to take and you robbed me of the chance to say goodbye to the friend that I loved so dearly. What's worse than that is that you opted to give her away. When we would ask why, the only explanation we would get was, "I sold her for a bag of chips and a can of coke."

I hated you for that. You stole her and didn't even have the courtesy to keep her. We agonized over the hole you made in our hearts and in our home.

It wasn't for another year later that we learned the truth. You decided to give our dog to your mother who lived in Florida. Even though we knew where she was, we were hundreds of miles away. Do you remember me trying to load her into the car when we were leaving? Do you remember me crying as I watched her chase our car as we drove back to New York? You may not remember, but I know mom remembers how much I cried. She saw how much of a hole Sabrina left in our hearts. As a result, she surprised me during Christmas with a puppy named Fritz. He wasn't Sabrina, and could never be, but I still fell in love. I slept on the floor next to him all night, determined to never let him be taken away from me. There were many times when Fritz was my only friend in the world as we moved to a new home or changed schools. Just as Fritz has always been there for me when I needed him, I will be there when he needs me. I found out that Sabrina passed away last year. It broke my heart that yet again I was unable to say goodbye to her. However, with Fritz, I promise things will be different; I will be there until the end. I will be a true friend.

After all of that, and so much more, I just didn't have it in me to forgive you. The mere thought of it was enough to make my blood boil. My hatred was insurmountable, yet my little brother was different from me. He was willing to try.

At first, I was shocked that Matt decided to get dinner with you, but I decided to be supportive of my brother and his decisions. I told him, "look, I don't want you to feel like you have to justify yourself to me, or anyone for that matter. If talking to him is something you want to do, I support it fully, but I simply don't have it in me to forgive him yet."

The path of forgiveness kept growing on the DeAbreu side of the family. My grandfather and my godfather spoke for the first time in nearly 20 years shortly after his birthday, which by coincidence, is also my birthday. My Godfather, my father's brother, has always been there for me when I needed him. I have grown accustomed to coming to him for advice. When he told me that he was speaking to my grandfather,

I was shocked and I asked "why." My Uncle Nick, my godfather, is not a man of many words, but he didn't need many to convey his point, "We are getting old, and the old man; well, he is really old now. He is my father, and despite what happened in the past, he is trying to change." I told him that he had given me a lot to think about, but I just didn't believe that people can change their nature. The past is real and it wasn't going to just go away. I can't pretend that it didn't happen, because then I would be denying my existence.

Now two people that I loved had forgiven someone that hurt them and I was still paralyzed. Hatred had rusted the door to compassion shut and move the handle as I may, it all felt futile.

March 2017:

Months had passed since I read his letter on my birthday and I still had not found the desire in me to make peace. My brother and father were getting along pretty well. My grandfather is even attending my cousin's sweet 16 in the summer. I'm not sure if they ever even met before. Then there was me, unable to forgive. My anger has not evaporated, it was still there. It was only locked away.

I decided to speak to Matthew again about how I was feeling.

I asked him, "How did you forgive him?"

Matt responded, "I didn't. You see, that all happened so long ago and I think it is time to bury the hatchet. I understand you and why it is hard for you to forgive him. I'm just tired of all the nonsense and I don't care about it anymore. Why don't you just grab dinner with him, he's asked about you. What's the worst that can happen?"

With a heavy sigh, I walked away and said, "I don't know, I'll think about it."

I thought to myself, *"Bury the hatchet? It feels like I'm giving it to him and hoping he doesn't swing. What reason could I possibly have to let him back into my life? Wouldn't it just be naive to believe that he has somehow changed?"*

Later in the day, I painstakingly typed out a message to my father asking him to grab lunch with me. We picked a date and now it was a matter of waiting. My stomach twisted in knots and my mind was chastising me, *"Why are you even doing this? This is a waste of time. Nothing has changed!"*

I battled with my feelings on the matter, but I ultimately decided it was something I needed to do for myself. I came to the realization that I deserved peace. I knew that if I decided to open that door, a lot of other people that I haven't spoken to will try to squeeze their way through. The thought of being obligated to listen to any one of them again sickened me, but I left my negativity outside when I walked into the Mineola Diner.

I watched him climb out of his Dodge Durango and walk towards the door. A part of me smiled and I hated myself for it. My mom would always do that to me. When I was angry with her, she would just tease me by getting in close and saying my name in a playful way. No matter how angry I was, she could always get a smile out of me and apparently, so could he. I bit my cheeks and choked it down. I walked over, said "hello" and lead the way into the Diner.

When I was a kid, he would always grab the back of my neck and steer me when we were walking. However, those days are long gone. I will not be lead on your leash anymore. I walked in and I asked for a table. The gentlemen seated us and I dived into my menu. I still wasn't ready to look at him, but I realized that it was childish, so I faced the man behind my menu.

When I looked, it wasn't what I expected. My father had aged. Although his age was evident in his salt and pepper beard, it was very clear to me in his eyes. He didn't have that intense look that would set me on edge as a child anymore. He seemed softened by the weight of the years and reflection. I could see pain and regret in his eyes. I could see that in his contemplation he asked the same question, *"What if things happened differently?"*

He didn't know what to talk about with me; it was like sitting across from a stranger. He spoke about his travels with my stepmom and half-brother, Leo. I always thought the term, "half-brother" was strange. How could I have half of a brother? He simply is my little brother, whom I am senior by 15 years.

A part of me always felt guilty for not being able to really participate in Leo's life. For that I am sorry little brother. Perhaps one day, when you are older, you will read my story and understand the depth of my heartache. I know it was selfish, but it simply hurt too much for me to watch him have another family. While he came home to a loving family every day, I came home to an empty house. Although my mother loved us very much, I didn't see her most nights until 9:30 pm.

My family always had to struggle to survive. We moved essentially every two years, while he had one home all this time. Times were always tight, but we found a way to get through it with a smile. We also have an older brother, "Emmanuel" my father's nephew, that my mom adopted after they divorced. Although we may not be brothers in blood, we are brothers in spirit and in our struggles. Manny is seven years older than me, so that means he is 22 years older than you! I'm actually laughing to myself at the moment, because I am 22 as I write these words. With each passing day I can feel my time slipping away from me, but you know what? I want to share an important lesson I learned with you, 'you don't have to be blood to be family.'

The next part was difficult for me. I finally found my voice, and said, "I know you have been asking about my college graduation, as well as, Papa. At first, I didn't want you there and there is still a part of me that thinks you shouldn't be there. However, everyone seems to be making an effort to rebuild the bridges we burned and I am willing to give this olive branch. I am inviting you to my graduation, but understand that I won't be spending that day with you. I will be spending it with Mom, Uncle Nick, and Aunty Nellie; they have always been there for me."

He nodded in agreement, "When you have the date and location just send me the information and I will be there." He grabbed the check and we parted ways. I gave him another handshake, and said "goodbye."

I found myself in a great deal of turmoil after our lunch. All the things that I wanted to say to him, not a word came out. I wanted to be angry, but I couldn't be. His eyes were just far too tired. I wanted to tell him, "You were wrong. I achieved everything you said I couldn't and I did it all without you." The words were crushed in between my teeth—his hair was just too gray.

I had to ask myself a difficult question, "How would I feel if he died and I never made peace with him?" That question has haunted me for a long time. The spiteful parts of me say I would feel nothing, but I know in truth regardless of my experiences with him in the past, I would still feel something.

This was the beginning of a long road, but if he was willing to take the first few steps, I could try. I came to understand that the man that sat across from me earlier today had grown from the man he was five years ago, just as I am no longer that broken boy.

As time went on my college graduation came and my father gave me another letter:

"Money will come, and go, but pursuing only money will perhaps leave us unhappy. Don't chase the bill, chase life."

I have come to find that the path to forgiveness lies in gratitude. The pain that I carried in my heart was the fuel that kept my fire burning in the darkest moments of my life. I poured every ounce of my being into improving myself and to proving to myself that I had value. When I was broken, it gave me a chance to rebuild myself. When I was lost, it gave me a chance to find myself. When I was scared, it gave me the opportunity to find the courage to keep fighting.

Thank you, father, for helping me find my resolve. Thank you, mother, for fanning my fire. I have learned many lessons from both of you, indirectly and directly. However, I think the most important lesson I have learned from both of you is to "be kind to all people, offer help when you see someone struggling, and fight when you really want something."

I am not a prodigal son, I am just a man that has learned that in forgiveness my soul will know peace.

I have come to accept that in life, we all experience pain, hardship, and heartache. You can decide to carry that with you your entire life, or you can simply let go. If your hands and pockets are already filled with negative emotions, it leaves you with little or no space for any of the good ones. For every bad experience we have, we can have thousands of great ones. I have learned that I should not dwell on the pain of today, but dream of the joy of tomorrow.

If you do hate someone, I understand how impossible the idea of forgiving them may seem to you, but the only person that suffers from hatred is the person who holds it. I was recently inspired by a story of forgiveness that far exceeds the realm of my understanding.

More Powerful Than "The Angel of Death"

There is a woman named Eva Kor. She and her twin sister survived the Holocaust. Her family was taken to the infamous Auschwitz Concentration Camp by cattle car, and within thirty minutes her family was destroyed. The Nazis identified that she, and her sister were twins, and they were then pulled away from their family, never to see them again. Twins were of special interest to the Nazis during the Holocaust for scientific experimentation. The reason being, when assessing an assumption utilizing the scientific method, you need a variable and control group. Identical twins served that criteria because they would be the most accurate representation of a control group. They were taken under the black wings of the "Angel of Death" Dr. Josef Mengele, and underwent inhumane and blatantly savage experimentations. All of this was in order to achieve Dr. Mengele's dream of contributing to an increased birth rate of the Aryan race.

Eva explained how they were stripped naked and starved. The photos are chilling; they were utterly emaciated and humiliated. The "Mengele twins" would undergo multiple injections of unknown substances without any regard to their survival. Eva reflected on a time when one of the injections she received made her deathly ill. Dr. Mengele himself came into the barracks and looked at her charts. He emotionlessly stated, "too bad, she is so young, she only has two weeks to live." In the weeks to come Eva battled her fever, but it would not break. In the documentary I watched, I saw her eyes grow more intense as she recalled upon a moment of lucidity she had while suffering from her unknown ailment. Eva remembered awakening in the barracks with a desperate thirst for water. The sink was at the other side of the barracks and she didn't have the strength to move, let alone stand. Unable to stand she fell to the floor. She began to crawl on the floor dragging her body towards life. She was so exhausted that she was fading in and out of consciousness. Yet, despite the hopelessness of the situation, she kept pushing herself forward, saying, "I must survive." After many attempts, she reached the water. Rejuvenated, she recalls feeling stronger for have reaching the other end of the barracks. With a new-found strength she began to recover. After another six weeks of battling, she finally broke her fever. To this day, neither she, or her sister, ever learned the truth as to what had been injected into them.

On January 27th, 1945, the Soviets liberated the 7,000 remaining prisoners of Auschwitz. That number makes my stomach wretch. Between 1940 and 1945, more than 1.3 million PEOPLE were deported to Auschwitz and only 7,000 were liberated. As children we fear monsters, but very few of us ever had to face the monsters we imagined. In the Holocaust, not even children were safe from the systematic annihilation of anyone that did not meet the requirements of Hitler's Aryan race. It has been estimated that nearly six million Jews were ruthlessly murdered by Nazi firing squads, gas chambers, disease, and starvation. In addition to the Jews that were murdered, millions of other people were killed in the concentration camps such as prisoners of war, Gypsies, and homosexual people. There are monsters in this world, and they just look like ordinary people. Humanity is capable of great evil.

Although we as human beings carry within us the capacity for hatred and evil, we also possess an incredible ability to endure the blights of the world with the power of choice. Eva and her twin sister Miriam survived the Holocaust. However, the rest of their family had been murdered by the Nazis. All they had left in the world was each other and despite enduring absolute despair, their struggles were not over. In 1987, Eva's sisters' kidneys failed. Miriam had been struggling with severe kidney infections for years and any antibiotic prescribed proved to be ineffective in combating the disease. Her case perplexed Israeli doctors, which resulted in them conducting a study on her. The doctors had discovered that her kidneys never developed into an adult size, a likely result from Dr. Mengele's experiments. Eva gave one of her kidneys to her sister and it saved her life. Sadly, Miriam had contracted a rare form of cancer that ultimately claimed her life six years later. She died in June of 1993.

Shortly after Miriam passed away, Eva had received a phone call that would send her deep into contemplation. A professor at a college in Boston had contacted her after hearing her speak at an event. He invited her to come speak at his college and requested that she bring a Nazi doctor. It was a bizarre and perhaps insensitive question to ask of her, but she considered it. She recalled of a documentary she had been involved with that had a Nazi doctor that was stationed at Auschwitz, Dr. Munch. She later got in contact with Dr. Munch and although he was unwilling to come to Boston, he invited Eva to his house in Germany.

It is important to note that Dr. Munch was acquitted of all charges of war crimes in the Nuremberg Trials because,

"Hans Munch was acquitted by the Highest People Court in the whole extent of the accusation . . . not only because he did not commit any crime of harm against the camp prisoner, but because he had a benevolent attitude toward them and helped them. He did this independently from nationality, race, religious, and political convictions of the prisoners." - Nuremberg Trials

I was interested to learn more about the interview since the documentary didn't go into it too deeply, so I used the resource: (http://www.jewishvirtuallibrary.org.) In the website's historical archive, I found a more detailed version of their conversation. When Eva arrived at Dr. Munch's house, she asked questions about Dr. Mengele because she had speculated that he was still alive after finding a statement about Dr. Mengele in a Justice Department Report regarding his son, Rolf Mengele. According to what was discussed in the interview, Rolf had come to Dr. Munch with the family attorney to ask him the hypothetical question of, "what would happen if my father returned to Germany? Do you think that he would be found guilty?" Eva had found it very suspicious for his family to make such an inquiry because Dr. Mengele's body had been found in Brazil in 1979, but oddly enough, his death was not confirmed until 1985. Dr. Munch shared this suspicion and the conversation grew more intense from there. Eva began to question him about the operation of the gas chambers and his role in it. Dr. Munch was responsible for certifying the deaths; he would look through a peephole to confirm that no one was moving after the chamber had been gassed. He wouldn't write the names of those the Nazis murdered, only the number of people that were killed on one death certificate.

After Eva's initial meeting with Dr. Munch, she described him as, "very kind and very considerate." This meeting inspired her to invite Dr. Munch to return to Auschwitz for the 50th anniversary of the liberation of the concentration camp in 1995. He agreed to attend. It was on that day that she did one of the most remarkable things I have read about in my life: she gave Dr. Munch a letter of forgiveness. The idea of forgiving a Nazi was bizarre. She did not know where to begin. Her English professor had been assisting her with expressing her thought, and correcting her grammar. Her professor pointed out an interesting issue while aiding her with the letter, "it wasn't Dr. Munch who hurt you, it was Dr. Mengele."

She suggested that Eva go home and imagine what it would be like to forgive Dr. Mengele. This proved to be one of the most challenging decisions that she has faced, but she realized something in her contemplation, "forgiving him made me feel pretty good, that I, the little guinea pig, of 50 years, even had power over the Angel of Death of Auschwitz."

She handed her declaration of Amnesty to Dr. Munch as they stood together in the Auschwitz Concentration Camp. I shared a piece of her declaration below:

"Look up to the skies, here in Auschwitz. The souls of millions of victims are with us, and I am saying with them as a witness, 'enough is enough. Fifty years is more than enough.' I am healed inside, therefore it gives me no joy to see any Nazi criminal in jail, nor do I want to see any harm come to Josef Mengele, the Mengele Family, or their business corporations. I urge all former Nazis to come forward and testify to the crimes they have committed without any fear of further persecution. Here in Auschwitz, I hope in some small way to send the world a message of forgiveness, a message of peace, a message of hope, a message of healing.

NO MORE WARS, NO MORE EXPERIMENTS WITHOUT INFORMED CONSENT, NO MORE GAS CHAMBERS, NO MORE BOMBS, NO MORE HATRED, NO MORE KILLING, NO MORE AUSCHWITZES"

Eva Kor's story was inspiring and almost supernaturally beautiful. After losing everything that she loved as a result of discrimination, racism, and dehumanization, she found the courage to forgive not only Dr. Mengele, but all Nazis for their crimes against humanity. She realized after coming from a time when she had nothing; the only thing she truly had was the power of choice. The Nazis took her family, her clothes, and her body. However, they could never take away her freedom to choose how she would feel. Fifty years after the liberation of Auschwitz, she stood side by side with a Nazi, and offered him forgiveness because she was no longer their prisoner, and she would no longer be a prisoner to hatred.

I will always admire her for the strength of her soul. Despite surviving the evils of humanity, her soul had the strength to give the world a message of love. Try to apply her lesson into your own life. We have all had people that we despised, but perhaps it is time to write your own declaration of amnesty. You never even have to give it to them. You can declare forgiveness for yourself, because you deserve peace.

Father, although you may not accept this, I forgive you. With age, I have come to understand that you are simply a man. All people have their regrets in life and I am sure you have yours, just as I have mine. I no longer wish to carry this burden of hatred on my shoulders. I also wish to relieve you of the pain I may have caused you.

Just as my little brother has taught me how to forgive you, I hope that perhaps you can learn from yours. We are simply getting too old and it is time to move on into the next stage of our lives. I want you to be there for all the big moments to come. Just like you, I will be married one day. I will be a father and I will make mistakes. This future is exhilarating, yet terrifying to me. Despite my fear of the uncertainty to come, I consider myself lucky because now I have: A mother, a godfather, three brothers, and a father to give me the advice I need. They will give me the advice I need to make me the best father I can be when my day comes. The past has been decided, but together, we can choose the future.

Chapter 10
LOVE

Forgiveness is the key that allows us to open the path to manifest divine love. There are many languages to love. However, our ability to communicate with them is hindered by hatred and anger. I once read in *The Art of Peace* by Morihei Ueshiba, "those who are possessed by nothing, possess everything."

I had to first remove the blockage to my true heart before I was able to give myself to another person. Ironically enough, the path to love is filled with heartache and difficult decisions. Perhaps one of the most difficult decisions I have ever made was to break the heart of another person for the sake of my own.

Letting Go:

Before I found the woman in the stars, there was another woman that I loved. Although our relationship came to an end, I do not regret any of the time I had with her. I do not regret ever loving her. I spent nearly five years of my life with her. We had battled through many difficult times together and shared many experiences together. What was once young love grew into familiarity; we were both accustomed to each other and the routines we shared.

As I grew older, I changed. However, it was still the same her. I was excited by the many new experiences I was having and all the things that I was learning through my voracious appetite to read. The books I read left me feeling inspired and ready to tackle the world, but she did not share the same goals as me. The more I learned, the more difficult it was for me to stay. As my feelings grew more distant, I felt an immense guilt that weighed heavily on my heart. I tried to love her and give her my heart even though we did not share the same goals. We were just two different puzzle pieces that were taped together in order to force the grips to hold. I blamed myself for not being able to give her the love that she deserved and craved.

I honestly believed that it was because I was so damaged that I wasn't capable of loving her, or anyone for that matter.

I abruptly reached my breaking point while I was at my desk in the office. As I ticked and clicked away on the keyboard, I would also listen to audiobooks. In this case, I was listening to The Alchemist by Paulo Coelho for the second time, because it was the one-year anniversary since I first read it. The most beautiful books are like a grand hall filled with doors. The door that you open depends on the key that you have. In the year since I read his book, my key had morphed and the teeth were to open a different door.

My heart burned inside of me, as I heard the story of how Santiago fell in love with Fatima:

"What the boy felt in that moment, was that he was in the presence of the only woman in his life, and with no need for words she recognized the same thing. He was more certain of it than of anything in the world. He had been told by his parents, and grandparents that he must fall in love, and really know a person before becoming committed. But maybe people who felt that way

never learned the Universal Language, because when you know that language it is easy to understand that someone in the world awaits you. Whether it is in the middle of the desert or some great city, and when two such people encounter each other and their eyes meet, the past and the future become unimportant. There is only that moment, and the incredible certainty that everything under the sun, had been written by one hand. It is the hand that evokes love, and creates a twin soul for every person in the world. Without such love, one's dreams would have no meaning, 'Maktub' thought the boy."

The passage caused me to have a panic attack at my desk, as I burst into tears. I only had one panic attack before this one. However, this particular one was of a far greater magnitude. My internal world plunged deep into the fog of war. It was a battle between heart and mind for my destiny. My mind argued, "she loves you, how can you throw away someone that loves you that much? You are just damaged, you need to try harder, you need to try harder." My heart wept, and said, "You do not need to 'try' to love someone, you simply do. If you end your relationship it does not mean that you never loved her; it means that you loved her enough to let her go."

I ran off to the bathroom as discretely as I could. I locked the door and desperately tried to get control of my breath. I faced myself in the mirror and asked, "What is the right thing to do?" My memories lead me to yet another book for the answer, Extreme Ownership by Jocko Willink.

The book teaches that a leader should take responsibility for the results produced by his team. If a team succeeds or fails it is due to the communication of the leader. In my frenzied state I came to the realization, "I must take responsibility for my feelings. I am not protecting her by hiding my true heart. Love is not an emotion you force, you are capable of love, so stop feeding yourself that excuse."

The next day, I made one of the most difficult decisions I have ever made. I broke the heart of someone that loved me. I tried to tell myself that it was the right thing to do for the both of us. I told myself that I wasn't happy and she deserved someone that could be happy with her. I was stealing her time by trying to be what she needed me to be. I ended up writing a lot of my feelings out on paper. I wrote down everything that was bothering me that I had tried to talk about with her in the past. She insisted that I meet with her so we could talk. Out of respect for our past, I met her later in the week for dinner. I shared with her my deepest feelings and what I needed for the relationship to work. Sadly, she didn't hear me. She only told me what I wanted to hear. With a promise for change, we decided to try just one more time. Unfortunately, that did not last long. We were grabbing at something that was no longer there. Within days of us getting back together, my Nana passed away. My Nana was the kindest soul to walk the face of this earth. She adopted my mother and her sister; she raised them as her daughters along with her other six children. My Nana and my mom grew up humbly. Things were always tight, but they always found a way. That mentality apparently carried down to the next generation because that is my family's motto, "don't panic, we will figure it out somehow." Although I had the opportunity to love and know my Nana, I never got to know my grandfather. He passed away long before I was born, but I knew of him through stories. My Nana and my grandfather had a deep and wonderful bond. My mother has had experiences that suggest that some love can even transcend the boundaries of death.

Whenever my Nana would come to visit, my mother would also see her father. She once told me of something that happened while in between a dream and reality. She saw my grandfather standing in the doorway of her bedroom and he spoke to her, "Where is mom?" My mom in her half-asleep state was confused, yet she answered the question, "Mommy is not here anymore Daddy, she went back to Canada." He whispered back to her, "okay, I am sorry to wake you, go back to sleep." My mother slipped back into sleep only to wake up conflicted in the morning, *"was it a dream, or reality?"*

On another occasion, many years later, my Nana had come to visit us. While we were sitting outside on the deck, we began to speak of my grandfather. My Nana was reflecting on how much she loved him, and in that moment, a monarch butterfly landed on top of her head. The butterfly rested on top of her head for a few minutes. We all looked at each other, our eyes saying the one thing that remained unspoken, "It's him."

When my Nana passed it was extremely difficult for my mother. It was also my first experience with death. The thought of never hearing her on the phone again crushed me. When my Nana said hello on the phone it was always, "Hello darling" in her gentle English accent. Every time I heard her say that, my heart would melt, and the biggest smile would come over me. Sometimes, I pretended not to hear her the first time, just so that she would say it again.

The one thought that gave me peace was, *"my grandfather has been following her for more than 20 years now. They have finally been reunited, and perhaps their souls can rest now."*

I expressed my deep sadness to the girl that I tried to love and she responded with four words. When she met my sorrow with four words, I knew that it was the end. I knew that I had not found the twin soul that was created for me. The realization pressed deeper on my heart when I thought of the love that was shared between my grandparents, *"I want a love like what they had."*

For one final time, I had to break her heart, with the realization that if I didn't do it now, it was only going to become more difficult to do. I faced her and with compassion I explained to her that this was the end.

I told her, "Do not give up on finding your true love, because you will love again. One day I will be nothing more than a distant memory when you are in the arms of the love of your life. I understand if you hate me, but I would rather you didn't. I think in time it will become clear to you that this was the right thing to do. We have just grown into two different people. We are on two different paths, so this is goodbye."

I finally had to take the advice that I had given to my friends so many times after a break up, "The world is a vast place filled with infinite opportunities. Yes, things may have come to an end, but who is to say that the love of your life is here in Long Island, New York? Maybe some people are lucky enough to find the love of their lives in their hometown, but if you do marry your high school sweetheart, or some small-town guy or girl; will you be happy? Or will you find yourself asking the question, 'What if the person I am supposed to be with is on the other side of the world waiting for me?' You will never know the answer, if you spend your time thinking about it. You have to go find her, she is out there, waiting for you."

Many of us stay in relationships where we are unsatisfied, merely because we are afraid of letting go of the person we are comfortable with. If you find yourself complaining to your friends about your significant other quite often, there is a much deeper underlying problem. You are always too young to simply accept your life as it is. If you are unhappy, stop talking about it and make some changes. You shouldn't be talking to your friends about things that bother you about your significant other. If you aren't able to communicate your feelings to them, your relationship is bound for failure. Despite how great things may be in the beginning, the passion will burn out if you do not attend to it.

If your relationship has evolved into something toxic, where every fight turns into a bloodbath, it is absolutely time to let go. In the course of nearly five years with my ex- girlfriend and my now accumulated seven years of total dating experience, I have never once raised my voice or directed foul language towards my significant other. If you love someone, you would never call them a bad name, because to attack someone's identity in an argument is more than demeaning, it's dehumanizing. To attack someone's identity is the most vicious thing you can do. If an argument ever grows into something physical, it is evident that person does not love you. Do not allow someone to attack your self-worth and blame you for their actions. You are a human being and you deserve respect. You are worthy of love. If you have ever found yourself in a situation when your relationship has devolved into domestic violence, just know that you are not alone. There are resources available to anyone that needs a way out of a relationship that has become abusive. You can find help at these links (Helptorestorehopecenter.org and safehorizon.org).

We are all deserving of love and it is okay to have high standards. You should never force yourself to feel something that simply isn't there. As much as you may try to lie to your heart, the truth will always be there. Sometimes in order to find our true love, we must let go of someone we once loved. She will always have a special place in my heart and I harbor no ill will towards her. I sincerely hope, from the bottom of my heart, that she finds someone that makes her feel invincible.

Omens Wait for No Man:

After closing the long chapter we wrote together, I was prepared to stay single for a while so that I could find myself. I thought that taking some time would help me identify the woman that I had been waiting for my entire life.

I never considered that someone may have already been waiting to find me. Luckily, they did. When I was single, Asvini finally had an opportunity to express her feelings to me. She told me that a part of her wanted to wait a little a longer, but another part of her told her to do it now. She explained that she had tried to be patient. She had been patient for far too long and something pushed her to act. When she confessed her feelings to me, I immediately confessed mine. Life is funny. Sometimes the treasure that you have been looking for has been in front of you the entire time. We agreed to take things slow because it was her first serious relationship in over four years and it was my first time being single in five. Although we both agreed to take things slow, before we knew it we had fallen in love with each other.

I remember she once told me that she went on an, "okay" date with someone before. Feeling confident, I reflected on that memory with her and told her, "The date that I take you on, will be the best in your life. Anything less than perfect is unacceptable. You will never have another 'okay' date if I have anything to say about it." She smiled wryly at me and accepted my challenge.

I had put a significant amount of planning into the date I had planned for us and I was excited when the day came. I met her at Molloy College and we were off to the train station. Our first stop was at the Museum of Natural History. I know to some of you that may seem a little boring, but I was there with a purpose. You see, Asvini was fascinated by space. She was a stargazer like me, so I decided to take her to see "Neil DeGrasse Tyson's Dark Universe" feature inside of Hayden Planetarium. When the lights went off, we were in the outer edges of the galaxy. As she watched the show, all I could pay attention to was the smile on her face. That smile filled my heart to the brim. One thing from the show did stick with me: two stars may fall into each other's orbit. With each passing moment, the two stars orbit each other closer and closer. It may take minutes, days, centuries, or millennia; but those two stars were destined to touch one another. When they did, it would cause a supernova.

With each passing minute of that day, I was falling more deeply in love with her. I already knew I was winning our little bet after watching her reaction during the show, but that was just the beginning of the day. We were starving after the museum, so it was the perfect timing for my next surprise. We were off to Chinatown, so I could take her to my favorite hole in the wall off of Pell St. She was blown away by how good the food was. This restaurant had the most delicious soup dumplings. I know some of you may think, "dumplings? How ordinary." However, you couldn't be more wrong. The soup was wrapped inside of the dumpling and was filled with meat. The broth was thick and rich and the meat was tender and flavorful. They would bring it out to you in the traditional bamboo steamer and it would also have steamed cabbage inside.

When you removed the lid, you would see the steam rushing out and the scent would overpower you. Without realizing it, your mouth started watering. MY GOD! These dumplings were amazing!

I had to show her the proper technique to eating these delectable treats so that she wouldn't burn her mouth with piping hot soup. You see the trick is to put it in your spoon and then poke a hole in it on the top. After that, you would gently open your chopsticks up inside of the dumpling to let the steam out. You would have to do your best to prevent the soup from spilling everywhere. *Frankly, if you don't eat them with chopsticks, you aren't really getting the full experience.* She popped it in her mouth and by the look of her eyes widening when she tasted it, I could tell that I had made another fan of this restaurant.

Afterwards, if she wasn't stuffed yet, I was going to be sure to fix that. I took her to Mango Mango. They have the best mango styled Asian desserts in the whole city. We laughed as we read the sign on the wall, "no outside food please, we hate the smell of our enemies." There were so many options, but ultimately, I ordered the snow-white mango juice with mango and red bean. She got almost the same thing except instead of red bean, she got the gluttonous rice balls. The dessert is served cold and it was soupy. I know it may seem weird to you if you are not Asian, but you should open up some new horizons. Often times it's the strange things in life that can make us the sweetest memories. At this point in the night she was absolutely glowing with joy, but I still had one more surprise for her.

We decided to walk off our very big meal and were having the time of our lives getting lost along the way. All the while we were lost I couldn't help but think to myself, *"As long as you are with me . . . I will never truly be lost again. . ."* I know I'm so sappy that you are probably cringing. However, I am an unapologetic romantic. While in stride, she suddenly came to a stop, "no way. . ." I looked at her perplexed, "What is it?" She then answered in disbelief, "The song that is playing right now, it is my mom's favorite song." Ordinarily, this may not seem too weird to most people. However, it was an extremely odd coincidence for a few reasons. One, she was in the middle of talking to me about her mom and was telling me that, "I know she is going to approve of you." Two, the song was in Sinhalese, a Sri Lankan language. Three, we were in Chinatown when we heard a Sri Lankan song. This was the first of many odd coincidences to come. These coincidences, or omens, were the first of many small signs of approval.

As we continued down our path, she started to get a sense as to where we were heading, but I refused to give it up until the last second. I had plausible deniability on my side, but I didn't even bother with a poker face because I knew she would see right through it. A few more minutes had passed and we reached the Rockefeller Centre Tree. She had never seen it before in person and it was always my favorite thing to do around the holidays. We both just stood there in silent wonder as we watched the lights on the tree and the show that happens on the Saks building.

After the show we knew our day was drawing to an end, yet we tried to make it last by stalling as much as we could. She was an excellent negotiator, "After treating me to the best date I have ever been on, I think the least I can do is buy you a cup of coffee." Again, I see that devilish smile that could make my heart melt, *"how could I say no to her?"* Before I could come to an answer, she was already grabbing my hand and leading me to the closest Starbucks.

A part of me wished that day would never end, but it was getting late and the time to depart grew imminent. I gave her a kiss goodbye and began my drive home. I was completely under her spell.

As we continued to date, I sent her a poem that I thought was beautifully written. It was called—

Soulmates
by Lang Leav

"I don't know how you are so familiar to me—or why it feels less like I am getting to know you and more as though I am remembering who you are. How every smile, every whisper brings me closer to the impossible conclusion that I have known you before, I have loved you before—in another time, a different place, some other existence."

Surprisingly enough, I had selected a poem by her favorite poet. However, about a month later, we were surprised again. We were speaking on the phone and reflecting on how funny that it was that out of all the poems I could have picked it was written by her favorite poet. She went on to tell me that she had all of Leav's books. At random she picked one of them off the shelf and decided to read it to me. The page that she opened to was, "Soulmates." When she told me what page she landed on she laughed to herself, showing the intimate piece of herself that she reserves for those closest to her. While she laughed, my heartbeat began to climb because she had not realized what I had. I said, "Soulmates, was the poem I sent you more than a month ago!" Both of us were at a loss for words, completely amazed by this seemingly impossible coincidence. She made a note of the date and time this strange occurrence happened. Today we still laugh about it. All I am saying is if that is not an omen, I don't know what is.

The omens do not come to us when we think we are ready, they come to us when the universe knows that we are ready. When you hear or feel the omens calling to you, it would be wise to listen. Although they call to you now, do not take them for granted because if you continue to ignore them, they will leave you. If life happened exactly when we thought we were prepared for it, there would be no challenge. There would be no opportunity for growth.

Twin Souls:

In the search for true love we must be patient and kind. The world is much bigger than the towns that we grew up in. True love still awaits even people who were married and got divorced. We all deserve to be loved and I do believe that there is a twin soul that feels exactly the way you do. They are also frustrated, exasperated, and doubtful that they will ever find their other half. If that is the case, you simply cannot risk feeling defeated by love. Your resolve must be unyielding. Otherwise, you will never find each other. If you have both given up the search, your paths will never cross. So for the sake of the love of your life, do not give up on them. It is your job to be searching for him or her so when the moment presents itself, you can say with confidence, "I have been searching for you all my life. It has been a long and difficult journey. At times, I felt there was no hope for me, but right now, in this moment, I understand why I had to search so long."

Although you must be patient in the search for love, you must also be bold. When the love of your life is right in front of you, you must find the courage to speak. If you are too afraid to share your feelings with that special person, you may lose your chance. Many times we allow the loves of our lives to slip away from us out of fear of rejection. I understand that the fear of not having your feelings returned may be daunting, but the pain of never knowing what could have been is far worse.

To those who feel that all they can find are players or people who ultimately end up hurting them, let go of your bitterness. You need to learn the greater lesson. Learn to raise your standards to the quality and quantity of love you deserve. You must first understand that we are only worthy of receiving of that which we are willing to give to another person. Do not expect a man or woman to sweep you off your feet with some grand romantic gesture if you are not willing to do the same. Do not expect someone to speak to you in the language of love when you demean them. Do not expect another person to understand you if you are unwilling to show them who you really are. I understand that opening up to another person may be difficult for those of us that have been deeply hurt by the betrayal of love in the past. However, closing yourself off from the world is not the answer. You must simply learn the greater lesson and become more selective with whom you share your true self. Trust your heart and your instincts.

You will know when the right person presents themselves to you. Do not force something that is not there and do not fool yourself into believing that you have found the one because it would be easier to settle.

Love is so much more than superficial attraction to external beauty. Love is a deep understanding of another person. When you look that person in the eyes, you can see the truth that hides beneath the mask they wear. When you stand there and truly see another person and feel how important they are to you, that is true love.

The Red String of Fate:

There is an old Japanese legend about a man who lives on the moon. At night he comes to earth in order to reunite kindred spirits by tying a red string around their pinky fingers. The pinky finger is significant because the ulnar artery has a thin vein that connects the pinky to the heart. It is believed that thin vein has an invisible extension that manifests in the material world and connects us to people we are destined to meet.

The red string does more than tie us to our soulmate. It ties us to people in life that we have something to learn from. *Have you ever felt that if you never met a certain person, your whole life would be completely different? I know to believe in fate may seem childish or naive. After all, they are only stories. I simply choose to be enchanted by the story because all stories, fiction or otherwise, have truths in them.*

I choose to believe in the red string of fate because I was born in Singapore and the woman that I love was born in Sri

Lanka. Through the twists and turns of fate, we have found each other in New York. We have both lived similar lives and endured similar hardships; we are even more alike in how we persevered to overcome them.

What choice do I have, but believe that my actions may have been guided by the hands of fate? When I look her in the eyes, what choice do I have but to believe that some encounters are perhaps predestined?

Feelings of Sonder
by Ethan DeAbreu

The song of oblivion is inevitable
The breath in my lungs will escape me
My vision will fade to black
Yet I do not fear the certainty of my demise

I have no fear of death
I fear the regret of not loving you enough
Regret of not asking for one more kiss
Regret of letting your hand leave mine

However, when I look in your eyes;
Regret is a far-off thought
I see past lives filled with love
I feel the warmth of you in my heart

If the song of oblivion is inevitable
Then let us dance into our endless night
One last kiss before we fade to black
Until the next dance my love

I will find you again

When you love someone, imagine that you are tending to a fire. Although the flames of passion may burn brightly in the beginning when unattended, a gentle devotion will ensure that your love burns forever. We are born to love, but raised to hate. In your heart you already have all that you need to love and be loved. You are complete.

Chapter 11
ROGUE

Perhaps one of the most significant discoveries in the course of human history, or rather, rediscovery, was the pigment blue. It may be difficult to imagine, but the color that has come to accent our night sky was once lost to time. The Egyptians are actually credited with creating the first artificial pigment, thus dubbing it "Egyptian Blue." Some of the earliest uses of the color date back more than 5,000 years in the paintings that are in the Tomb of Ka-Sen. Ka-Sen was the last Pharaoh of the First Dynasty. The color had signified a relationship with life and the divine. However, when the Roman Empire collapsed, it was lost for nearly 1200 years. In the 1700s the only available blue was extremely expensive because it was created by crushing blue gemstones.

Oddly enough, it was actually on one man's quest for gold and immortality that lead to the rediscovery of the color blue. Heinrich Diesbach was a Berlin chemist, dye maker, and aspiring alchemist. Although he was unable to convert metal to gold or find the elixir of life, he created something more valuable than gold. His discovery has been immortalized in some of the greatest artistic masterpieces in history. In a time when the color blue was so rare that artists would have to negotiate with their patrons for the use of a single drop, he serendipitously discovered "Prussian Blue." His rediscovery of this heavenly color sparked a renaissance of the once lost hue and "Blue Fever" spread and infected the hearts of the world. Diesbach believed that the soul of a living thing could be transferred into a new vessel. Although he may not have achieved the immortality he envisioned, I believe that the soul of his work has transcended death. The pigment that he created would later become the quintessential essence of Japanese art. The color blue would inspire some of the greatest artists in history to create their masterpieces. While we may mock those that pursue the impossible, sometimes greatness lies at the edge of madness and genius.

In my room three scrolls hang from the wall over my bed. Together they depict my favorite piece of art, "Kanagawa Oki Nami Ura." Artist Katsushika Hokusai created the woodblock print of "The Great Wave off Kanagawa" during the Edo period of Japan. I have always been captivated by this image since I first saw it in the textbooks. The image is veiled in controversy and secrets that an untrained eye would miss. Although this is one of the most famous pieces of Japanese art, it was condemned when it was first created because it is in fact a print and not a painting. The Japanese viewed this style of art as uncouth and coarse because woodblock prints could be mass produced. They believed that prints did not elicit the emotion that a painting captures. Furthermore, it was not designed in a Japanese purist form. Katsushika Hokusai gleaned inspiration from European styles.

Despite a lack of internal support, the print went into production around the 1830s. However, Japan was notoriously isolationist during those times. Their ports were only open to China and Korea; they refused to engage in trade with the Europeans. Japanese ports didn't open to the Europeans until nearly 1860. When they did, the prints finally reached the western world. The print of the Great Wave was enchanting to the Europeans because of its realism. Van-Gogh has accredited Hokusai's work as an inspiration for the color and style of "The Starry Night."

Hidden amongst the spellbinding allure of the azure cresting wave there is a secret that often goes unnoticed. There is a mountain hidden amongst the waves. The picture is actually a part of a series of prints, "The 36 views of Mt. Fuji." If you look closely at the center, you will notice the image of snowy peaked Mt. Fuji blending into the raging sea. Many people also assume that the wave is a tsunami. However, in fact, it is a Rogue Wave. A tsunami typically arises as a result of an underwater earthquake, whereas a rogue wave in its nature is an unpredictable, catastrophic force.

Why is all of this important?

The image of the powerful wave rising out of the ocean was inspiring to me in a strange way. There is a theory that suggests that Rogue Waves form by taking the energy from ordinary waves and consolidates it to form one incredibly large wave. To me, it almost seems like the wave rises as a challenge to both the skilled fisherman and majesty of Mt. Fuji.

The wave swells and crests in defiance to its surroundings. It rebels against the fisherman that took its presence for granted; it compiles the energy of all those willing to give, to grow, and surpass the mountains that once stood far above them all.

Through a symphony of chance and courage, one wave exceeds the realm of the ordinary and achieves something teetering on the edge of the divine. I like to view the rogue wave as the manifestation of passion. We may live our lives as gently as we can, moving back and forth as cosmic forces push and pull us. However, some of us will never be satisfied with following the tides. I'm tired of doing what is practical; predictability is overrated. I was born Rogue.

An Unexamined Life:

There is a Japanese adage that goes, *"A frog in the well does not know the sea."* How does one become a rogue wave when they are barely in a puddle? Many of us make broad opinions about the world based off of limited experiences. We think that we understand the ways of the world, but in reality, we haven't even left the confines of the town we grew up in, let alone the country. We are trapped in the well of tradition and practicality. We simply do things because that is the way they have always been done. We have been conditioned to believe that risk is bad and that it should be avoided at all costs. Sometimes playing it safe is the most dangerous way to live your life. Although you may not see it now, perhaps you will understand the gravity of regret when you face the end.

As yet another year draws to an end, I find myself in the application process for a new job. Things didn't quite work out at my last place of employment for a few reasons. The biggest problem was that I couldn't fake passion. There were other factors that involved me leaving, but my boss told me before I left, "you are very passionate about the marketing team and every time you have the chance to write an article, you light up. I just don't see that same passion for accounting."

I didn't say much, realizing that it was the end of an era. I couldn't argue because he was right. In a matter of fact, I actually laughed to myself thinking how oxymoronic what he said sounded to me.

He wants me to be passionate about making Excel Spreadsheets... I thought I was showing passion by working hard, pitching new ideas, and learning as fast as I could, but apparently not. Apparently, I should have just followed the advice of my senior and "kissed more ass." Actually, no, I don't think so . . . I have too much pride to kiss ass for advancement. The problem with that firm was that I saw nothing to aspire to become. Did I want to become a senior accountant too? To have the honor bestowed upon me to send emails at midnight to my coworkers and clients? To have the honor of working 80 hours in a week for the price of 40? Did I want to have to come into work on Saturday for free as well? No, I didn't want any of that. I was already completely burnt out trying to hold onto my dreams as I begrudgingly gave my time to a firm that preached family, but practiced fratricide. I despise hypocrisy more than anything.

He was right. I had absolutely no enjoyment in my life when I spent my time at a firm where everything was so contradictory. It was a place where people that I didn't even know that well were ready and willing to slit my throat for advancement. If you watched Game of Thrones, you can say that I got Jon Snow'ed. It was a pretty vicious Jon Snowing at that. Regardless of reason or circumstance, I am here today on the search for a new career. When I return, I will not be so naive again.

Sometimes I fantasize about having an aneurysm at my desk as I click through an endless cycle of personality questionnaires and painfully repetitive questions such as, "If you were in the situation, which of the following actions would best represent how you address it?"

So far, the fruit of my efforts could only produce humiliatingly low intern wages for a career that I am qualified for.

Yeah sure, I'll work for $11 an hour to pay my student loans in the next 1,000 years or so. No problem. Is it arrogant to know you are worth more than $11/hr? Is it arrogant to want to be paid fairly for the Bachelor's degree you earned? I honestly don't know anymore. I can't even be envious of my friends that are working because they are all miserable. While the most time I ever clocked in for a week was 84 hours, I have friends that are crushing those records working 90- 95-hour workweeks. The worst part about it is that they accepted that this is just life because 'it's normal.' Maybe I'm just too idealistic. Perhaps life really is nothing more than working some job you hate for 50 or 60 years and just dying. I keep getting the advice from others that I should just settle on something. I should just follow the path and in ten years I could be making $150,000 a year. The problem is that money really doesn't motivate me. I really don't care about making that much money if I'm miserable the entire time.

Currency fluctuates up and down in value every single day in relation to other currencies. However, the value of time can only increase. You can always amass more income. Yet, you can never earn more time. Time is just too precious to gamble away hoping to get a promotion or simply working at a job you hate. In an absolutely perfect world, I wouldn't be tied down by the need for money. I would have left long ago, but the world is far from perfect. In this less than perfect world, I sit here behind the same old luminescent blue light that hypnotizes and sedates me. I am no longer playing the keys like one of my grand composures. I am merely ticking and clicking as we accountants do. I am simply waiting for some HR manager to read my cover letter and resume. I am waiting for them to make an on the spot assessment of my character before they go home and play with their cats. I am ready and willing to begrudgingly sell my soul to the highest bidder. I just wish I wasn't such an idealist. Maybe if I wasn't, I wouldn't be so bitter.

A Life Worth Living:

Come on, you didn't really think that I would give up in the eleventh hour!

No, I am afraid that mindset is simply not going to work here. My family's motto is, "don't panic, we will figure it out somehow." I am not about to prove the phrase that has kept us afloat for so long to be wrong. My life is not meaningless and I don't have to be anything I don't want to be. To accept the path and "settle" as others have been advising me would be the most fundamental betrayal of everything that I have ever believed in.

Life felt like it had no value before because I failed to look within to see the value. I failed to take the time to evaluate what was truly important to me. I failed to understand what it took in order for me to achieve true peace in my lifetime.

When I imagine being a wealthy man, it doesn't really involve having exotic cars, mansions, and thousand-dollar shoes. If I were to achieve true wealth in my lifetime, I would simply be a traveler of the world. For me to be truly wealthy, all I would need is my camera, a laptop, and a partner to travel with me as I collect the most beautiful and inspiring stories in the world.

I wish to serve the world, not the interests of a company. I can't be ready to throw in the towel because I believe in my mission. I know that if I work hard enough, I will be able to break through the glass box of practicality that I have found myself in. If I give up today, I will never know my true potential. I refuse to be another walking corpse. I will not be the person that will show up to work on time for the next 60 years and be buried in another 3. I simply value my life far too much to accept that this is the end. Admittingly, I may have to take another job, but it is not the end. It doesn't make me a hypocrite to work a job; I am only a hypocrite on the day that I stop working on myself.

The Great Death-Muga

Do you remember your first memory? I know it may seem like a strange question, but I find it even more bizarre when people don't have an answer. When exactly did we develop a sense of self?

I remember waking up for the first time. I was at the bottom of a flight of stairs. I was utterly perplexed. I started speaking, but I didn't know what I was saying. As I sat there, unaware of what exactly it was that I was doing, someone brought Matthew and placed him next to me. Although I did not know him, something inside of me did. His name bubbled up to the surface of my mind. Confused, I muttered, "Matthew." I leaned in to touch his face and I became aware of my arm for the first time in my life. I didn't have complete control of my body quite yet as I moved, so I could not stop. He then bit my hand and I felt pain for the first time. I jumped away and stood up. All I could mutter were two sentences, "he bit me!" and "where is mom?" I wandered the house looking for a "mom", but not quite knowing what it was.

I have heard that it is common for our first memory to be one of pain. Although I experienced pain, I woke up before Matthew bit me. After that day, my consciousness faded away again and I didn't wake up until I was in some strange place.

My mom sat me down on some cheetah print pillow . . . and there was a man with a ponytail . . . and he was wearing denim jacket . . . Definitely the 90s... The next thing I know there is a lion on my lap. I was completely mind blown! I was speaking to this "mom" person again and repeatedly I said the same sentence, "mom it's a lion. Look, it's a lion!" I knew that they heard me, but I was interested in the sound of my own voice, so I kept repeating myself. It was so strange to become aware to what my own voice sounded like. As I was petting the cub, it bit down on my hand. Personally, I think it's funny that my two earliest memories involve me being bitten by something. I gasped and repeatedly stated, "He bit me!" The funniest thing happened after that. Since the small lion cub bit me, the only logical thing to do was to give me an even bigger one for the photo! Then after that it is all a blur again . . .

When your consciousness forms, it's like being born again into the world. This is your true birth. What these experiences have taught me was that the ego can die and reincarnate. The ego is our sense of self and identity. At some point in our lives, we woke up decisively and we have continued to make decisions while using one frame of awareness. Imagine, at the age you are now, that although your body is alive, your consciousness dies again. Would it be terrifying or liberating?

My fascination in the death of "self" has lead me to read various philosophies about the meaning of life and the ego. The philosophies that resonated with me most deeply were from Japan. Japan is the birthplace of history's most fearsome and elegant warrior. I am talking about the samurai. While many fear death, it was the duty of the samurai to actively seek it.

The samurai lived their lives in accordance to Bushido, "the way of the warrior." "bushi" refers to the warrior class in Japan and "do" is used to say "the way of." The foundation of the precepts of Bushido can be found in three philosophies or beliefs. These three beliefs, Shinto, Confucianism, and Zen Buddhism held the most influence in Japan. In regards to the samurai, Shinto was the teacher of sincerity, harmony, and honor. Confucianism focused on loyalty and courage. Lastly, Zen Buddhism was the teacher of self-reliance as well as separation from the self. These philosophies were essential to creating the Yin and Yang of a samurai.

The samurai was both the beautiful cherry blossom that would one-day wilt and the tempered steel of a katana that hungered for honor though battle.

Although Bushido is "The Way of the Warrior," a samurai by the name Yamamoto Tsunetomo wrote, *Hagakure, the Book of the Samurai*. This was a fair representation of the "Soul of the Samurai." Even though the book was never intended to be published, there is a great deal of wisdom in the pages. For the purpose of this chapter, I am going to focus on the teachings of Zen Buddhism in relation to his journey. It was through the practice of Zen that Yamamoto died for the first time at the age of 22. During his first death, Yamamoto held a ceremonial funeral of his ego when he achieved the state known as "Muga." Muga is a spiritual state where the mind and the body disconnect and we rely on instinct instead of thought. It is believed that the ego, which is simply who we are in our current state, is nothing more than an illusion. The ego is nothing more than the mask of "self" that we wear; it was created through culture and experience. If we learn to remove our ego, we will experience what Zen Buddhist refer to as Daishi, "The Great Death." In death we are free of our ego and we are able to act without the inhibitions of thought and the prejudices of opinion.

> *"The way of the Samurai is found in death."*
> *- Hagakure, the Book of the Samurai*

The word "samurai" comes from the word "saburai", which translates to, "one who serves." In order to truly serve one's master, a samurai must die. When the ego is present, he will never truly be able to devote himself to his master. Devotion is the word that is critical to understanding the heart of a samurai. They are devoted to their master because honor dictates that they be the weapon that serves his will. Their devotion exceeded the realm of death. Before it was banned in 1663, it was not uncommon for a samurai to commit junshi, a ritualistic suicide, to follow their master into the afterlife. The way of the samurai is found in death because the samurai is the embodiment of death. He willingly seeks death of the ego so that he may face the inevitable death of the body with a heart of stone.

The Way of Creation:

We all have our own path in life. However, that does not mean that we cannot learn from others. I have learned a great deal from books, yet knowledge without application is meaningless. I feel that the way of the samurai resonates so deeply with me because I innately adopted many of its principles in order to survive. When my heart broke for the first time, it was a death of my "self". I did not reject the pain I felt, but accepted it and continued down my path. My heart has broken many times and with each death, I leave the part of me that died in the past. I detach that part of me from that "self." I have had to sacrifice many times in order to survive. I have had to work jobs that damaged my pride. I had to learn how to let go of the mindsets that held me back and the excuses that justified me standing still.

We often give ourselves less credit than we deserve. It is in human nature to be robust and resilient. However, we often choose to reject our true nature out of self-pity. Sometimes it takes desperation to jolt us out of pity. When you have no other option but to execute, you will. The reason why so many of us are resistant to making the changes that would improve our lives tremendously is because there is no urgency. It is a difficult thing to achieve, but we must stop making excuses and surrounding ourselves with people that accept them. We are capable of so much more. I think it is about time to start acting like it.

What separates the majority of us from achieving our goals is conviction. Just as the samurai devotes himself to his master, we must devote ourselves to our mission. When the samurai failed or dishonored himself, he would be obligated to commit seppuku. Seppuku is a ritualistic suicide where he would disembowel himself. For the record, women could be samurai too. They were also obligated to commit seppuku, also known as hara-kiri, in order to redeem their honor. While these practices are now archaic and outdated, when you really think about, if you are not devoted to your dream to the point where you are willing to die for it, you will never achieve it. It is comparable to seppuku of the soul. I do not want to die a martyr to my own ambitions.

We have fallen in love with the idea of being successful, but in our hearts, we hold disdain and fear of the work that it will take to create it. How many people have you see with the social media biography of "Entrepreneur?"

Posting motivational quotes does not make you an entrepreneur. How many people spend more time taking photos of their gym outfits or flexing rather than actually working out? Buying expensive workout clothes does not make you an athlete. We spend more time massaging our egos than devoting ourselves to the process. Though we may update our status or buy expensive things, true progress tells no lies. We are the direct reflection of the hard work we put in.

"Men with contriving hearts are lacking in duty."
- Hagakure, the Book of the Samurai

I have spent a great deal of time thinking about "the way" and what it means to me. It was difficult for me to group my many interests into one category, but the answer that I have come up with for now is, "the way of the creator." I feel that my purpose in life is to create things, both tangible and intangible. For example, I love to write and I love photography. So, in order for me to remain true to my way, I must actively seek and complete these activities. My creative soul craves to create change in the world as well. When I look out at the world, I see a lot of suffering. I can tell myself, "there is nothing that I can do." However, that answer would mean that I surrendered myself and my abilities to the world. If a solution does not exist, then the responsibility to find one will weigh on my soul.

Although we may try to paint the world as black and white, I will always persevere to see it in color. *As you already know, color can be lost as result of negligence.*

By chance and circumstance, I was brought into the world. However, I do not have to live by chance. As a human being, my potential is infinite as long as I choose to believe that it is. Limits only exist in our minds. For every obstacle that stands in my path, I will find or manifest my own solution to overcome it. In order to advance on the path that I have laid out, there is one thing you must never do. You must never accept any circumstance as permanent. A creator does not see things for what they are, but rather, what they could be.

Sometimes in order to create, we must first destroy; just like life, and death, all of creation and destruction is a cycle. If you wish to walk the path of the creator, you may need to destroy the piece of you that refuses to see opportunity.

We often spend more time complaining about our circumstances, rather than doing something to fix it. You must destroy the negativity within you, there is no space for doubt in the heart of a creator. In order to follow "the way of the creator" you must create. There are too many people that "think" about doing something and not nearly enough that actually begin. You don't need expensive equipment to be creative; everyone has to start somewhere. Every move must be strategic. When I didn't have a laptop to write stories, I bought a notebook and pen. When I didn't have a DSLR camera, I would use my phone. When I couldn't afford a gym membership, I did calisthenics or ran outside. We have make the most of what we have in order to earn the right to have something more.

It is also important to know that a creator creates for their own satisfaction. You may work diligently on a project and you may think it is the best thing you have ever done. However, there are others that may not agree with you. Some people may even discourage and demean you for the product of your project. The opinions of others are not necessary for the creator to elicit joy and satisfaction. Although the support of others is always welcomed, true happiness for the creator can be found in the process.

Currently, I co-host a podcast with one of my best friends. It's called, *The Morning Lift*. At the moment, we have a grand total of eight episodes and maybe 25-50 followers. We do not rush progress or over concern ourselves with the numbers because we love doing what we do. Although some people criticize and discourage us from continuing, we persevere. It doesn't matter if you do not have a large audience in the beginning; success doesn't come overnight. What matters is that you believe in the mission you are sharing with the world. If you wield your words with conviction and sincerity, your message will eventually reach the hearts of others. Despite my small following, I have had several people message me and tell me, "thanks, I really needed that episode." It is the little things like that inspire me to keep working. This shows that my words can reach the world.

Live life with passion that crashes with the ferocity of a rogue wave. Live life with the same devotion to your mission as a samurai. In the death of the ego, we may see the path hidden by the superficial. In the removal of the self, we become free.

Chapter 12
Utopia

The opposite to fear is love and the opposite to hatred is empathy. The difference is often lost on most people. Empathy is the bridge that can gap all suffering because it breathes compassion.

Some may call me a fool, but I believe that utopia is possible. I can see a future without war, without poverty, without starvation, and without injustice. To many the thought of utopia translates to nothing more than useless idealism. We tend to accept the ethos that, "human beings will always disagree, and as such, there will always be war." Why? Why is this the only way that we can be? Have we truly become so detached from the world and each other? It doesn't matter where you are from or what your religious beliefs are; all humans are capable of speaking the universal language of compassion. The world will know peace when we learn to speak to one another with compassion and love rather than hatred, fear, and sympathy.

We lose the ability to empathize when we choose to judge before we understand. We are all born knowing the language of compassion. However, like all things, if we do not practice what we know, we forget. I have learned many lessons in compassion by watching my mother and brother. They are both kind and sincere souls; they both motivate me to become more fluent in the language that unites us all.

My mother and I are similar in the way that we experience emotion. We both feel things very deeply, to the extent of feeling another person's pain by looking into their eyes. Behind the eyes you can see the true heart of a person. We may elect to conceal the pain we feel, but you cannot hide from someone that has experienced the same pain. Life is suffering and from suffering we grow. My mother and I carry our burdens in the same way. We both wear a mask of strength. We walk with confidence and we speak in terms of practicality. If we spoil our facade the world will see exactly how easily hurt we are. This vulnerability terrifies us. The heart of an empath is subject to overflowing if we do not regulate what we feel.

Despite our efforts to conceal the depth of our pain, some things are just too heartbreaking. These feelings pass through the membrane of the walls we put up.

I have a great deal of empathy for my mother because I know her story. I saw through her mask of strength when I was young, but rather than pull it away, I adopted my own. My mother without a doubt resonates with her sign as a Leo. She is a lioness. She is fierce, yet nurturing. She has consistently pushed herself to the extent of her abilities in order to protect her family. Although times were tough and we had many close calls, we always found a way.

My mother's compassion has always been something for me to aspire to reach. Even when times were tight, she would always find a way to give. In a recent incident, we were at the supermarket when we overheard a woman complaining about an elderly woman begging for money outside. She threw a tantrum in front of the store manager and demanded that she be removed from the premises. When she walked away, my mother was furious, "It is the holidays! How can someone be so horrible?!" She had helped the woman that was outside a few times and she found the complaint to be deeply disturbing. The woman outside wore a white winter coat and pink gloves. Her face was kissed by the wrinkles of age and her eyes were a soft blue. As we walked outside, we saw the manager of the store approaching to ask her to leave. However, before we could intervene, another man gently grasped the woman's hand. We paused as we watched something wonderful. The man said a small prayer for the woman and gave her some money. I am not a religious person, however, there have been times when I have said things that were religious in order to give another person comfort. The faith of religion does not resonate with my soul, yet I can understand and see the peace that it can give another person. After the young man walked away, my mother also approached her. Almost as if an old friend, she gave her what little money we had on hand.

I am sure that when my mother looks at this woman, she sees my Nana. She can't help but feel a deep pain for her because had it been her mother begging on the streets, her heart would have broken. In the golden years of our lives, we tend to regain the gaze of innocence that we had as children. The old woman's eyes were warm on this windy winter day. We watched her walk away and it was if she had disappeared with the breeze.

I know seeing her breaks my mother's heart, because it reminds her of the difficulties of her childhood and the times when her family could not afford food. When we would eat dinner, she would always tell me, "when I was your age, we had to eat every grain of rice. Nothing could go to waste, so you may not leave the table until you clean your plate." That lesson has carried with me my whole life and is the reason why I never waste food. This is the reason why I grow irritated when I watch my friends carelessly throw things away. In the face of comfort, we take the simplest, but most important aspects of daily life for granted.

Blind Eyes:

We may choose to close our eyes to the suffering that happens around us, but that does not mean that it goes away. I have been to the city many times and I see the way the homeless are treated. It has always brought me deep emotional pain. They are treated like animals; no one pays them any regard. People can simply walk passed them and not feel a thing because they have been desensitized to their environment. What infuriates me more than anything is the air of arrogance or superiority that people have towards them. People often say, "I work hard for my money. You just laze and bum around." It is judgment like that which makes us forget the language of compassion. We must never judge that which we do not understand or know with certainty. You do not know the reason why someone is homeless. Being homeless does not give you the right to treat them as less than you.

According to the statistics gathered by the Coalition for the Homeless, in the fiscal year of 2017, "129,803 homeless men, women, and children slept in the New York City municipal shelter system. This includes 45,000 homeless New York City children." You also have to take into consideration that the number is probably higher than what the data collected, because some of the people that are out on the streets do not check into shelters. Some of the leading causes of homelessness in NYC are the lack of affordable housing, domestic violence, and hazardous housing conditions. It is ignorant to assume that everyone who is homeless is in their position due to laziness. Do you understand how ridiculous of an argument it is to suggest that nearly 130,000 people in NYC are homeless simply because they didn't work hard enough? Anyone of us can become homeless; it is a situation that demands more humanity.

Imagine if you lost your job, and despite your many efforts to get a new one, you are still unemployed after four months. How secure would you be? Imagine if your significant other was beating you every night, to the point where they nearly killed you. Could you imagine the strength that it took for them to leave? The homelessness situation needs to be addressed and it begins with us empathizing with the people that had the misfortune of losing their home. They are not animals; they deserve to be treated with compassion.

Typically, I will not give money to people if they ask for it. However, I am more than willing to buy a person food if they are hungry or provide clothes if they are cold. I remember one time I was on line to buy a metro ticket when an older woman decided to loudly ridicule a man who had no shoes on because he asked for money. She decided to go on a rant about how difficult her life has been and that he should stop being a bum get a job. She wanted me to agree with her, but I stepped off the line. I walked towards the man and I gave him $5. This was all the cash I had on me. I told him, "you don't deserve to be spoken to like that; better days are ahead." He thanked me and said a prayer to bless me.

The homeless have been treated so badly that some of them are no longer able to trust others. One night I was in the city with my friends for class and I had been having the luckiest day of my life. Everywhere I went, I kept getting things for free. I had the pleasure of enjoying three free cups of coffee, an ice cream, ramen, donuts, and a train ride. I was so pleased to be having such a wonderful day and come the end of the night my friends and I found ourselves in a Dunkin Donuts. It was the end of the night, so the cashier just gave us a huge bag stuffed with donuts. We were all thrilled to have some late-night treats, but then we saw a homeless man walk inside. He asked the cashier if he had any donuts he was going to throw away. The cashier didn't even have the courtesy to look him in the eyes. Emotionally muted, he said, "no, now get out." The man was hurt and angry. He said, "please! I'm hungry, I know you guys throw them away at night! Please, just give me a few and I'll leave." The cashier angrily repeated himself, "No, now get out of my shop you bum!" The man stormed out of the store and my friends and I followed suit shortly after. As we walked outside, we saw the man digging through the trash bins for his next meal. My friends started to walk ahead of me, but I couldn't move. Only Bobby saw how much the situation bothered me. He said, "go on, I see that you want to help him. I'll wait up for you."

I smiled and was grateful, that at least he understood what was going through my mind. I walked up to the man, as he threw some rancid scraps of food on the ground. I spoke to him gently and said, "excuse me sir, I was in the shop earlier when you asked for the donuts. I have some extra ones if you would like." What happened next I wouldn't have expected in a million years. The man grew violently angry with me. He said, "What do you think I am?! Stupid?! You don't think I know that you did stuff to them?! I'm not dumb!" There were some additional inflammatory words that he said that I am opting to not include. I was completely awestruck, but then I was threatened. He made a step towards me, but I put my hand out and said, "I am sorry, I didn't mean to upset you. I swear that I did nothing to tamper with these donuts. I am sorry that I disturbed you. I am going to walk away now and you will never have to speak to me again. I'm going to leave these donuts here in case you change your mind." As I walked away from the man, he continued to shout insulting remarks at me, but he did not pursue. Bobby and I shared the mutual look on our faces of, "well, that just happened." After a few moments I broke the silence, "look, I'm not upset that he reacted like that. I am just upset that his trust has been so broken that he thinks the worst of people. You and I both know that I meant him no ill will, but sometimes things don't go according to plan. I hope he decides to trust the donuts I left him over whatever he may find in the trash."

I understand that some people do horrible things. I know that there are people that scam people into giving them money. However, we have to give all people the benefit of the doubt. I want to believe that the good in the world far exceeds the bad. Misfortune can befall any of us, so rather than walk away from those in suffering, make an effort to help.

Luck:

If you ever have the opportunity to be spontaneously kind to another person, then take it. Sometimes life sets you up for a moment, where you can make a difference in someone's life, so don't be afraid to act.

One morning while I was driving to college, I received a phone call. I generally don't answer while I am in the car because I like the quiet of the drive, but for whatever reason, I decided to pick up. On the other end my friend was hysterically crying because she had been in a car accident. When she told me where she was, I couldn't believe it, she was just off of the exit I had just started to take.

When I got on Robert Moses Parkway, I saw her jeep on the side of the road. I pulled over into the shoulder when I got a chance and walked in the mud towards her. She had rear-ended the car in front of her when traffic suddenly came to a stop. The jeep wasn't totaled, but the bumper was resting on the tire so she couldn't drive.

I had to make a decision in that moment. If I stayed any longer with her, I was going to miss my classes for the day. I chose to communicate with my professors and explain the situation at hand. Most of them were pretty understanding. It was towards the end of the semester, so it was not uncommon for kids to be getting into "car accidents" and their "third aunt, twice removed" passing away. Fortunately for me, I had a good rapport with my professors, so I suffered no real consequence other than having to do a little extra work to catch up. When I saw how upset she was, my conscience wouldn't let me leave her. I told her I would cheer her up with some breakfast, so off we drove to the nearest diner. At the time I was so broke because I had been helping out at home with the bills. I was essentially living paycheck to paycheck with the little money that I could make each week.

However, she needed a little pick me up, so I didn't mind treating. By the time we walked out of the diner she finally had a smile on her face again and my job was done. I drove her home and went to college to catch up with a friend that took notes for me.

It was by sheer dumb luck that I had the opportunity to do something kind for a friend. I left twenty minutes later than I normally do on that day. Although it seemed that nothing was going as planned that day, sometimes you just have to take each day as it is and live as kindly as you can.

About a year ago, I had been in a similar situation as her. As I was driving to college, my car broke down on the highway. My first car was a 2001 Nissan Altima, a four-cylinder car that ran on three. Not only did I have to drive it with two feet, it was also an automatic. Even when I braked, I was constantly feeding it gas, otherwise the engine would give out on me. It was constantly the source of my depleted bank account. I would often joke about how "Lucina" could always tell when I had money in my bank account, because that's the exact moment when she would break. Despite the fact that she was constantly falling apart, I decided to name her Good Luck Lucy because the first letters of license plate were "GLL."

Lucina is her proper name though. Together, the two of us had rather miraculously survived for 35,000 miles over the course of a year and half. Unfortunately, she acted up and left me stranded in the middle of nowhere with an overheated engine in the middle of February. This irony was not lost on me.

I called a few people to help me out of this situation. At first no one really could come in to save the day. By my fifth attempt, I reached a friend at college who drove about 30 minutes out of her way to help me out. When she arrived she even had chocolate, because, "chocolate is good for the soul." Whenever we are fortunate enough to receive kindness from someone else, it is imperative that we remember it and pay that kindness forward when we have a chance.

Magokoro:

I grow frustrated when people express their sympathy when something terrible occurs in the world. This is because sympathy is not compassion, it's pity. Your sympathy is entirely inconsequential to another person because it lacks sincerity. Without sincerity one cannot truly understand the heart of another person. Sympathy is a hollow word that expresses no deeper understanding than, "Wow, that's unfortunate for you. I'm glad that it didn't happen to me." I know that may sound bizarre to some people. Yet, sympathy is nothing more than feeling bad for another person and to feel bad for another person is to pity them. It is unfortunate that thoughts and prayers are not enough to change the world. If they were, we would have seen the end of war. Children would no longer die from starvation; we wouldn't choose to profit off of disease. We cannot save the world if we choose to pity it. Sympathy lacks commitment and thus the ability to create change.

The word "Magokoro" is used to convey sincerity in Japanese. the etymology of the word signifies "absolute heart and mind." True sincerity can only occur when we experience life without the weight of our egos. When you sympathize with the misfortune of another it is to inject one's personal feelings about the event rather than understanding how the other person must be experiencing it. When we remove the ego, the only feelings left to consider are of the ones of the person that was hurt. When we only consider their feelings, we can achieve a deeper level of understanding.In enlightenment, we have the capacity to experience empathy. This is the alignment of heart and mind. While wielding the light of empathy we possess the sagacity, and poise, to illuminate the greater veracity of the world,

"Before the imaginary lines we drew in the sand and the arbitrary terms we used to define our existence, we were simply human."

When you are able to recognize that we are all human, it eliminates the barriers that live in between us. In the removal of the ego, you can see the hearts of others and connect with them by speaking the language of compassion. Train yourself to see with your heart and you will be able to see what lies behind the eyes of others. You will be able to understand them. My eyes have adjusted to the dark and so has my soul. Now I can clearly see that beneath the facades we all front, there is deep sadness and suffering. At the very core of our humanity we crave connection and validation that our existence matters. Although we live in the generation that fosters the greatest amount of resources for connectivity, we are more disconnected than ever. We only see the superficial and barely scratch the surface when it comes to meaningful connection. We then start value ourselves on measurements of the superficial. We allow ourselves to become dulled by the feeling of inadequacy.

When I look people in their eyes, not only can I see what they are trying to hide, but I can feel it in my heart too. I am not the type of person that typically sympathizes with others, but I can certainly empathize with the burden they carry.

When you can see someone is struggling to carry the weight of their burden, greet them with compassion and love. Even if you only relieve them of their burden for a moment, that is still a single moment where you made the world a better place for that person. I was once on line at the supermarket and I could see that the cashier was disgruntled. She was an older woman, probably close to about 55 in age. Her hair was in a messy bun and her eyes were brown. Her eyes gleamed with anger, but on the inside, I could see frustration and anxiety. I knew that she had no problem with me, but the problems of her internal world were slowly bubbling to the surface. When I came to the register, she did not greet me. Instead, she began haphazardly bagging my groceries. I decided to just meet her intensity with kindness. I put a smile on my face and from my heart I said, "Good morning, thank you so much for bagging my groceries, I really appreciate it." She quickly responded, "Yeah, no problem."

Although she tried to hide it with a coarse response, I saw her smile for a brief moment. She began to whisper under her breath about how tired she was, so I broke her train of thought and whispered back, "Don't worry everything will be okay." She finally looked up at me and I smiled as kindly as I could to her. Her eyes started to fill with tears, but she quickly wiped them away, and with a shaky voice said, "thank you."

At the time, my heart was also heavy with feelings of uncertainty and fear. Yet, when I saw the suffering of another person, it allowed me to escape myself. I was able to focus my attention on the present moment, rather than the pain of the past, and the anxiety of the future. In the moment when I spoke to her with kindness, we were both relieved of our burdens. I have heard people say that "you can never really tell what's going on inside the head of another person," but I think that those people are unwilling to see. We can all make the burdens of another a little lighter. With love and empathy we can work towards a better tomorrow; empathy is the bridge to gap all differences. Compassion is the language that we all speak. Now face the world with courage and embody the changes you wish to see in the world with kindness in your heart. The greatest sympathy I feel is for people with hearts ignorant to empathy.

The Humanist Revolution

The "Humanist Revolution" is a project of a lifetime that I have only just begun. Although I align myself with many different social causes such as Feminism, Black Lives Matter, LGBTQ, and climate change initiatives, I feel that dividing the energy amongst different causes is creating a losing situation. Our voices are never heard and our grievances are never addressed because we are all shouting over one another to say who has had it the worst. The ideologies that support these causes begin as pure, but then deteriorate into something unrecognizable because of differences in opinion internally. Great social initiatives fail to consistently gain traction because they are not gathered in unison on the issues at hand.

Before I associate myself with any other "ist" or "ism", I view myself as a humanist. That being said what is a humanist? What is this neo-humanism? I consider myself a humanist because I believe in the advancement of humanity as a species. For us to grow and evolve as a species we must stand together to address the inequities of the world. We need to greet all hatred and prejudices with unconditional love and reason. We need to stop viewing each fight for social justice as different and systematically address the grievances of the people of the free world. Not only will we finally stand a chance in the battle for social justice, we will win.

It is extremely disappointing that in the 21st century we still argue about whether or not a woman is equal to a man. We still argue whether a woman has the right to do as she pleases with her own body. Feminists fight for social and economic equity. They fight in order to smash through the glass ceiling and be acknowledged for the value that they contribute to society. Is it impossible to understand that women didn't get the right to vote until 1920? Does a law make something right or wrong? Or does culture? Haven't some laws been later found to be unjust? Although I do not think that the majority of men hold the archaic view that men are superior to women, there are still very apparent barriers that exists to prevent the progression of women in leadership. When you are privy to the subtle sexist symbolism in the media, then perhaps you can start addressing the larger issues.

Furthermore, we as a species fail to acknowledge the damages brought on others by prejudices throughout the world. In the United States, the Emancipation Proclamation abolished slavery in 1865. However, Jim Crow Laws which discriminated against people of color were in effect until 1964. Is it really that difficult to understand that centuries of oppression could have ripple effects into the modern world? These prejudices have been sustained by our leaders and exist in the hearts of those ignorant to empathy. Today we can turn our backs on people in suffering and refuse to accept refugees because, "all Muslims are terrorists." A strikingly shocking number of people still believe that Barack Obama was a Muslim. They frequently use that incorrect assumption to assess his character and his former position as President of the United States. We invoke nationalism by designating a scapegoat that we can collectively and blindly direct our hatred towards. Just as Adolf Hitler rallied the Nazis to commit crimes against humanity by scapegoating the Jews, Gypsies, and homosexual people; today, we are doing the exact same thing. Sure, you may argue that we don't have concentration camps like the Nazis did, but exactly how far away are we from that sort of thinking? How much more fear must we be fed until we are willing to steal the liberties of others in order to protect our own?

One of the most critical components to war is dehumanizing the enemy. Today we battle with ISIS, a terrorist group that has massacred the innocent for the sake of extremist religious dogma. However, we fail to acknowledge that the views they fight for are in the minority in the faith of Islam. Many of us refuse to acknowledge that all religious sects have their extremist components: Christianity has the KKK, Buddhism has the Ma Ba, and Muslims have ISIS. The problem with ideology is that it can be misinterpreted. Why can't we all acknowledge that at the core of all religions, they all try to preach love and compassion?

Or is the world really just that black and white?

Furthermore, I grow increasingly frustrated when people argue in the opposition to the reality of climate change. They argue that climate change does not exist despite the vast amounts of data collected and tests conducted by experts in the field that support its existence. We live in a world where beliefs are more important than facts. Perhaps one of largest national embarrassments in recent times is when the United States refused to sign the Paris Agreement. The agreement supported the initiative for all parties in the United Nations to make a global effort to reduce emissions and build a future towards cleaner energy. 174 out of 175 nations signed the agreement. However, the United States rejected the agreement because it was a "bad deal." The world has been screaming at us with drought, forest fires, record breaking earthquakes, and hurricanes. Yet, we as a species fail to collectively acknowledge the threat at hand. I do not understand the opposition to making the commitment to reducing our carbon footprint on the world. Even if you don't believe in global warming, which is an observable reality, you cannot deny that pollution exists in the world.

According to Plastic Oceans, which is a social initiative keen on the removal and prevention of man-made pollution in the ocean, "more than eight million tons of plastic are dumped into the ocean each year." Many of the plastic items we use are for single usage. One prime example of this is plastic grocery bags. The problem with plastic is that it is not biodegradable; it has to go somewhere after we dispose of it. If we burn it, it pollutes the air. If we bury it, it pollutes the ground. With all of this in mind, if we dispose of it in the ocean, what will happen? Plastics have destroyed ecosystems and lead many animals to die unnecessary deaths.

If the animals or our environment are not enough to persuade you to consider climate change, you need to then think about self-preservation.

The will to survive is instinctual to all animals. Yet, humanity's willingness to fight for self-preservation exceeds them all. Do you remember the hydrological cycle from elementary school? The simplified cycle goes as following: evaporation, condensation, and precipitation. This means that the water that evaporates from our oceans is the same water that rains on our homes. This is the same water that we drink and bathe in. Although the water we drink goes through different levels of sanitation, it is currently impossible to completely remove all plastics that dissolve into our drinking water. Have you ever caught a drop of rain in your mouth? Next time you do, make sure it is not acid rain before opening your mouth. Even if all of this does not resonate with you, can you at least acknowledge that humans have a negative effect on the environment? Can you at least admit that we could probably find a way to more efficiently utilize our resources?

If it makes me a fool to believe that there is more good in the world than bad, then let me die a fool. Perhaps it is time to start rehumanizing the world? We are all capable of looking passed the veil of the superficial and seeing the greater truths. I am tired of reading about innocent lives being lost due to the evils of humanity; I'm tired of hearing discriminatory language. Most importantly, I'm tired of believing I'm helpless.

All revolutions begin with a single voice and if the message rings true, it can grow into thousands or millions. Have the courage to hope. Together we can change the world.

We need to tear down the walls of ideologies that divide us. We need to remove the ego and see behind the mask. I am calling for revolution. We are humanity and the only way we can preserve it is by standing together. We can either be the match that illuminates the world or the one that burns it to ash. Let these words strike you and ignite the fire in soul. Your choices shape your reality, take ownership of the world you have created.

Chapter 13
VISION

For the first time in my life I may be in need of glasses and it causes a small twinge of sadness to pinch my heart. My eyes have always made me different from everyone in my family. I would often laugh to myself when I would imagine the genetic combination that made me on a Punnett square. I felt lucky to have traits with a low frequency of occurrence. Isn't marvelous how seemingly impossible the odds are of us being born? We all exist by sheer random chance, but I don't suppose we have to live that way.

Both of my parents have black hair and brown eyes. They are also blind in their own special ways. My mother is short sighted and probably wouldn't be able to recognize from ten feet away without the aid of her glasses. My father is farsighted and can only really perceive me at a distance. Matthew is funny because he can't even recognize me from five feet away! Me on the other hand, I have always been the odd one in the family. I have brown hair and dark green eyes that have a gold rings around the pupils. I have also always had exceptional vision, 20/15, and the running joke is that I have "hawk eyes" because I am good at perceiving a target far in the distance. I always liked that my eyes were different. Did you know that only 2% of the world's population has green eyes?

I have always trusted my vision, but the more I work in accounting, the blurrier my sight becomes. The things that were familiar to me, the targets I set my eyes on, are just blending in with the background. I am afraid of wearing glasses because I feel that they will not be able to restore the image of my vision. I fear that it will only ease the pain of losing something precious to me. So for that reason, I will go on without for the moment. Perhaps my eyes are only strained and need a few moments to adjust. However, if I keep forcing my gaze on excel spreadsheets, I most certainly will lose my vision.

I feel that the majority of the world is vision impaired. These people depend on the sight of others in order to see the path ahead. I'm simply not okay with the idea of following another on a path that I cannot perceive.

How can I trust that the vision of another is true and not a mirage? I have always trusted my eyes to see the path ahead, but if I do lose the light in my eyes; I'd rather go searching in the dark for my own answers than follow the crowd towards an unknown end.

Visions of Prometheus:

I'm dreaming again...

It's so strange to close your eyes in your dreams... Although my perceivable world is lost in darkness, I still feel alive. The breeze of the ocean is carried by the sound of a cresting wave. I can feel my heart relax and I'm overcome by a sense of peace as the mist of a crashing wave kisses my forehead. It's funny how much we can miss when our eyes are open if we aren't looking for the right things.

With a deep breath, I opened my eyes and I took in where I was because I knew that my time in this place was going to be short. I was sitting cross-legged on a rock that towered out of the ocean like a pillar. There was no other land insight. From my perception, it appeared that I was in the middle of the ocean. There were other pillars of black stone emerging out of the ocean with each passing second. I could feel the vibrations of my heart as I traced the pace of my breath. My heart felt as if each beat was separated by a matter of minutes. The midnight sky above was gentle and grey clouds lingered in the sea of stars. As I focused my attention towards the infinite ceiling above, the aurulent light of the moon reflected on a figure flying towards me. As it approached and circled me, it became clear that I was in the presence of something marvelous. An enormous stone-gray dragon gusted it wings with force of a monsoon, but perched itself on the pillar across from me with the elegance of a falling feather. Its presence invoked a deep feeling of wonder. It sat on a pillar slightly above mine. I looked into its sapphire blue eyes and it felt as if he was looking right into my soul. The incredible beast straightened its posture and spread its wings. In doing so he blocked the light of the moon and cast a shadow over me. He suddenly leaned forward and roared.

Blue fire poured out of its mouth and wrapped around the pillar I was sitting on. The azure flames climbed far beyond the height of pillar and surrounded me in a brilliant icy blue blaze that grew into the sky like a spiraling tower.

I was not afraid . . . how could I be? . . . I was enchanted. I stood up and stretched my hands out to edge of the flames. They weren't unbearably hot; the wisps flickered from a lukewarm and gentle fire. I traced the path of the spiraling flames with my eyes as they *stretched into the edges of heaven. There was a small opening in the towering flames above me and I could see the eye of the moon peering in at me. I reached my hands towards the sky, but then pulled them back towards a warmth in my chest. When I looked into my cupped hands, I was holding the same azure fire.*

When I awoke from my dream, I felt a deep longing for where I had been. I was overwhelmed by an unfathomable sense nostalgia for a place that never actually existed. Although I felt a spiritual anguish that desired a vivid understanding of what I dreamt, I also felt a sincere gratitude in my heart. It may have only been a dream, but it seemed so real to me. It was one of the most beautiful things I have ever seen. I had this dream nearly four years ago, but when I focus my attention on the details, I can find myself in the same place. I am able to remember the feeling of holding the fire close to my chest. At the time, I do not feel that I completely grasped the meaning of my dream, but today I think I do.

Allow me to set the stage. At that age of 17, I always had the belief, which was tucked away in the corner of my mind, that life would change the moment I was "discovered" by someone who saw my value. There was a quote that was omnipresent in my thoughts, "When the student is ready, the teacher will present himself." I felt ready and I was waiting for my teacher; I wanted someone to unlock my latent potential. I wanted someone to see something great in me that I was incapable of seeing myself. However, that person never came. That feeling grew into a nihilistic cynicism and I had come to believe that I was naive for thinking that I had something inside of me of any worth. Despite my doubt, I continued to pour my efforts into improving myself.

In my dream of the dragon, I was entirely mesmerized by the unperceivable beauty that was alive and happening around me. I secretly wished to myself, "I wish that I could make something that beautiful." Reaching towards the flames was the same feeling an artist must feel before picking up a paintbrush. I felt a desire to grab what was in front of me, but I was unsure of what I had the capacity to create. More than that, I was unsure if I even had the right to try and create something. When I turned my head to the sky, I just realized how small I was in comparison to the dragon, the ocean, and the infinite universe above me. I reached towards the sky in desperation; I wanted to understand my place in the world. When I asked the universe to show me my place in the world, it told me to look within. I felt the warmth and familiarity of the flames that danced around me in my chest. As I grabbed towards my heart, I saw that the same beauty that mesmerized me *existed within in me.*

Why do we spend so much of our lives waiting for the permission to live? We simply cannot afford to go on romanticizing what it would look like in the moment when life truly begins. We must let go of the day dream of some cosmic force that intervenes in our lives to save us from the burdens of the mundane. I'm tired of daydreams and I'm tired of waiting for change to occur. The time for action is now; we cannot live our lives in earnest hoping that someone else will come along and help us achieve a lifetime full of aspirations. We can only truly begin our lives in the moment when we realize that we are complete as we are. We do not need to rely on fate to provide with the perfect circumstances we dream of. When you take ownership of your life, you realize that you can create anything.

Astra Inclinant, Sed Non Obligant:

"The stars incline us, they do not bind us"

Right now, in this moment, you are free. I refuse to surrender my will to the fatalist. Choice is not an illusion, limitations are. More often than not we give up on an idea before we fully explore it. This form of self-sabotage is utilized to preserve the ego; it provides the foundation for us to say, "well, at least I tried." Perhaps you let go of a dream too early, maybe you thought you tried. However, when you reflect on it now, did you really use all of your power to make it come true?

Even if you tried and failed, ask yourself, "am I really satisfied with finality of my failure?" Did you fail after trying many different approaches? Or did you give up after one approach failed? I understand that it may feel like opening an old wound to answer these questions, but perhaps it will help you realize that the scar was not as big as you had remembered. It is all too common for people to write off their failures with the phrase, "well, it just wasn't meant to be." I am just not one of those people, I can appreciate the romantic appeal of fate, but I refuse to believe that I was destined to fail at something I was passionate about. If you truly have a love for what you do, you will go to the ends of the earth to achieve it. Failure is simply part of the process. We must overcome our failures with an unshakable resolve to achieve the end goal.

I was conditioned to believe that I was failure by those closest to me. That crippling label of "failure" felt like it was branded on my heart, but I was okay with it. I felt broken by the world, but that label reminded me that I had a purpose. The pain reminded me that regardless of my current circumstances, I was still alive. It is because they called me a failure that I was determined to work harder than everyone around me. Every test, every game, and every rep was a competition against both myself and everyone else. I realized that the path to freedom was in self-leadership. In order to be a leader, you must have a vision. When I was at my lowest, the only place I could look was up. I have always been climbing the mountain with the conviction to achieve a better reality. In despair and heartbreak, I learned how to dream. My dreams were what saved me from falling into depression; I clung onto the only hope I had. I held onto the vague belief that, "things can be better."

It wasn't much, but at the same time it was all I had. I was tired of suffering and seeing those I loved the most suffer. I needed to take control; I needed to start fighting back. Every time I fell, I crawled to my knees and found the strength to pull myself back up. The reason why I needed to become a leader in my own life is because my family needed me to be strong. My mom has always told my brother and I this, "Ethan you are my pillar of strength, you have always had the will to fight. I draw strength from watching you persevere. Matthew, you are my heart. Looking at you soothes my soul and calms me down. Without the two of you, I would have nothing." I couldn't crumble, because if I did, the whole thing would fall to shambles. Together, we have fought as a family. After enduring the wrath of entropy, we remain unconquered.

I found the strength to fight because I believed that, "If I can make things better for me, I can do it for them." I want to be the sword that cuts their chains, not the anchor that weighs them down to the ocean floor. The only way things could ever change was if I committed to the process. When failure is not an option, you have no choice. You must execute.

There is a poem that I often read when I feel myself slipping. Perhaps it will be of some help to some of you.

Invictus
by William Henley

"Out of the night that covers me,
Black as the pit from pole to pole,
I thank whatever gods may be
For my unconquerable soul.

In the fell clutch of circumstance
I have not winced nor cried aloud.
Under the bludgeonings of chance
My head is bloody, but unbowed.

Beyond this place of wrath and tears
Looms but the Horror of the shade,
And yet the menace of the years
Finds and shall find me unafraid.

It matters not how strait the gate,
How charged with punishments the scroll,
I am the master of my fate,
I am the captain of my soul."

Lucid Dreaming:

What if all of this is a dream? Maybe we are just stuck in a nightmare. Maybe we are forever chasing after some elusive paradise that formed in our minds. Sometimes it can really feel that way. No matter how hard we will ourselves forward, the thing we are *chasing after just seems to get further away. We can either endure the nightmare or wake up. In our submission to our fears, we willingly let go of hope. In waking up, we do not solve the root of our fears. We only run away from it. If these options do not appeal to you, there is a third . . . you can become lucid.*

Did you know that you have the power to control your dreams? For once, I am not speaking metaphorically, but I suppose it could be taken that way as well. In your dreams, you can become aware of the fact that you are dreaming. This state is referred to as, "lucidity." Once you become lucid, it is like walking a tightrope. Once you are aware of the fact that you are dreaming, you have to be sure that you don't get too excited at your realization or you will wake up. However, you must focus on staying conscious. If you allow your attention to slip, you simply fall back into your dream without any control. The more you practice maintaining your awareness in your dreams, the better you will be at sustaining it. When you do, the possibilities are only limited by the extent of your imagination.

My ability to lucid dream was cultivated through mediation. When I was young, I would have pretty intense nightmares and night terrors. Some nights I would wake up in cold sweat and others I'd jump out of my bed and start running. In my nightmares there was always something out to get me; I was powerless to defend against the evil. Mediation provided me with the capacity to control my mental landscape. However, when I surrendered this capacity while under the pressure of immense stress, there were repercussions. Mediation proved to be a double-edged sword for me. It was exciting to dream so vividly, but it meant my nightmares were just as vivid.

My first lucid dream was the result of a nightmare. I was running, as I always was, and no matter how much effort I put into running faster, my body felt heavy. My legs felt like pillars of lead being dragged on a jagged path. My perception of time became lost and the world lagged around me as fear filled my heart. As I ran from the figure in the darkness in pursuit of me, I questioned myself, "Why? Why can't I move faster?" That question led me to realize that I was dreaming. The sensation of not being able to run faster became a trigger to me in my dreams. This would always help me realize that this nightmare was all in my head.

Whenever I realize that I am dreaming, the first thing that I want to do is fly. In order to fly in your dream, you have to give yourself that ability and believe that you can do it. One moment I was frantically running for my life and in the next, I was flying into the sky without a care in the world. I was weightless; I could simply take off and leave the burdens that anchored me down. Until you experience flying in your dreams for yourself, you will not be able to imagine or understand the peace I felt. For the first time, I was free.

I have spent my life chasing after that sensation and it has led to a question that I will spend the remainder of my days searching for an answer to, "How can I free others, if I cannot free myself?" The only answer I have for the moment is, "live your life as if it were a dream." I will choose to walk the tightrope on the edge of lucidity and obscurity. If I lose my concentration, I will fall back into the fog of slumber. Everything is on the line, everything I ever wanted is on the other side. This time I will refuse to let it slip further away. This life is my dream and as long as I take the reins away from fate,

I have the autonomy to decide. I believe it is possible. I will work passed the limits of my mortal boundaries and persevere in order to achieve something extraordinary. Live life with intention and you can be free.

Manifestation:

Vision is only the first component of leadership. As a leader, it is your responsibility to move heaven and earth to achieve the future you have foreseen. Many people confuse talking about their ideas with others with actually making progress on their goals. To have a great idea is a wonderful thing, but it is meaningless unless you work to achieve it. Do not be fooled by your ego into believing that you have accomplished something by achieving praise from bragging to those around you. Popularity, praise, and pride, are not progress; they are distractions.

My first significant opportunity to lead others was at Molloy College. As freshman do, I attended the club fair and learned enough about each club to satisfy my interests. I attended the inaugural meeting of the Business and Accounting Club with a couple of my friends after the club fair. I immediately saw an opportunity that waited for me in the future. I turned to my friend Bobby and said, "This time next year, I will be the president of the club."

Bobby understood me and how serious I could get, so he laughed and said, "Don't you mean King?" My close friends often tease me in that way because I have a tendency to become pretty intense when I have eyes set on a target. I returned a devilish smile to my good friend and said, "of course." Surely enough, as the year went by, I involved myself in every club activity and became an expert. I had to learn as much as possible if I was going to have a chance to be voted in as club president. I had a vision for the club and I saw how much influence it could have on campus and for the students.

After one year's time, I felt ready to take the lead in the club. If I had not, I would have waited another year. I believe that there are times when it is better to be patient and wait for when you are ready rather than rush into something halfcocked. I am comfortable and willing to take risk in my personal life. However, I was not willing to risk the success of the club if I was unsure that I was ready. I was voted in as the president by a landslide for my Sophomore year. I spent most of the summer before the next semester strategizing and wondering how I could bring the greatest amount of value to the club. In my first year as president I learned the trade and made an effort to connect with my students, and other business club leaders. I hosted a wide variety of events, and maintained an excellent rapport with my students and the other campus leaders. The critical aspects to my leadership style were: reflection, empathy, critical thinking, creativity, and sincerity. I often stayed long after the meeting times to talk with the underclassmen.

I would often give them advice and would even help them study. Some of my favorite events that I did from my first year were: The Elevator Pitch Competition, Peanut Butter and Jelly Time, and a Board Meeting with the NY Mets. The basis of what an elevator pitch is founded on the hypothetical position of you being in an elevator with the CEO of a company. As the elevator ascends from the bottom floor, to the top floor of the building, you have one minute to pitch to the CEO why he should hire you or promote you. This situation may not happen exactly the same way in real life, but it is certainly useful to have your elevator pitch ready for a job interview. I knew that my introverted students would be hesitant to participate in this challenge, so I created a cash incentive and shared my pitch in order to give the students direction. Even if I wrote the entire pitch for another student, it wouldn't matter.

Even if you have the best pitch in the world, but you cannot effectively articulate it, you will not succeed. It was important to me to help cultivate their public speaking ability and in doing so, their confidence. The fear of public speaking has consistently been ranked amongst people's top five fears. However, having the ability to perform in social settings may have an impact on your earning potential in your career. I had to push them out of their comfort zones and I provided workshops for them to enhance their ability to perform under pressure. When the day of the competition came, I invited some of the business professors to help me decide on the winner in order to remain unbiased. I could see that some of my students were visibly anxious about giving their pitch, but I spoke with them individually in order to help them conquer this fear. Then I spoke to all of my students as a whole in order to reassure them that this a learning environment and that we are all here to have a little fun and to improve ourselves. I reminded them of how far they have come in the past two weeks of preparation and that regardless of whether they win or lose, they have obtained a new skill that will be with them for the rest of their lives. As we went around the room, some of the students had been hesitant to give their pitch, but myself and the rest of my students would encourage those who were anxious to just give it a go and have fun with it. In a room of 45 students, every single one of them gave their pitch. When we selected a winner, the room roared with applause and energy. Maybe it's just how I choose to remember that day, but I can honestly believe that not a single student held an ounce of bitterness towards the victors.

An important pillar in my life is charity and as such, I tried to incorporate it into the club. Peanut Butter and Jelly Time was an event that my team and I created in our Philosophy in Leadership class in our freshman year. The premise was really simple, but the impact and community outreach was extraordinary. The Mary Brennan Inn would take in the homeless, so we had the idea make them sandwiches in order to help feed the hungry. We went around town to ask local businesses to sponsor the event and we gathered funds from club budgets in order to buy all the supplies we needed. When we went live with our event, we set up tables in the middle of the busiest building on campus and watched as people came up to our tables to spend their time making sandwiches. It is amazing how such a simple idea can leave such a meaningful impact when it is acted upon. When I looked into the eyes of the students who opted to volunteer their time to make a few sandwiches, I saw compassion and pride.

We had a few people that loved the idea and took on the ambition to make the most sandwiches out of anyone. One student ended up making thirty PB&Js! For few hours we brought together ordinary people that were strangers to each other in order to work towards a greater good. We shared many laughs and a lot of positivity, so I decided to bring this event back through my club. In our first year sponsoring this event through the Business and Accounting Club we made more than 400 sandwiches for the Mary Brennan Inn. Each year after that we were determined to make it bigger and better.

The last event of my first year was the board meeting with the NY Mets. This event was the signature event of my club and was viewed as the reward for a year of hard work. A former member of the club is the daughter of the Vice President and Controller, Leonard Labita. We capitalized on this connection to get tickets to the game as well as the opportunity to sit with the executive team of the NY Mets as they gave us career and life advice. At the end of the event we would be able to participate in a Q&A and ask them anything we wanted. They were extremely considerate to offer time out of their busy schedules to sit with some budding college youths and give us perspective. After the meeting we would sit and enjoy a game! We celebrated a year of hard work and achievement with some tailgating and baseball.

At the end of the year I decided that I had not finished achieving the vision I had seen for the club and humbly requested from my students that I would be allowed to lead the club for one more year. Although there was an election, no one ran against me. They respected my ambition and were also curious to see how far I could take things.

Round 2:

I had been given the opportunity to explore my imagination in order to create something meaningful for others. This was the opportunity of a lifetime and I was not going to waste it. I decided to push myself to think bigger and outside of the box. This mentality inspired me to pursue the creation of the student chapters of the IMA (Institute of Management

Accountants), and FBLA (Future Business Leaders of America. The creation of the IMA was my main focus. It allowed my students to attend professional networking events each month in order to perhaps gain an internship and to become more comfortable with talking to strangers.

As a leader, it is important to understand that you cannot achieve everything on your own, so I delegated the responsibility to filing for the creation of FBLA to my Vice Presidents. It was a matter of killing two birds with one stone. While I delegated the work to them, it opened space in my schedule and allowed me to train students to ultimately become the leaders of the club when I retired. FBLA allowed my students to compete in competitions for academic merit. Some of my students even placed amongst the top three in their respective categories of testing for the state. I could not have been prouder of them. In the creation of these student chapters, I provided my students with something of value and created something that will exist long after I leave the club.

I reaped many benefits from the IMA and met many interesting people. The two most notable experiences I had at the IMA was meeting the CFO of Nathan's Famous Hotdogs and interacting with employees of Canon U.S.A.

Sometimes in order to create an opportunity, all you have to do is ask politely. On a rainy Thursday night, I attended the monthly IMA meeting. I had been quite tired from the day of work and classes. Furthermore, the weather contributed to my desire to simply go home. Despite my inclination to relax, I decided that it was my responsibility to attend these meetings, so I put on my suit and my best smile. As I went around the room, my advisor pointed out to me Ronald DeVos, the

CFO of Nathan's Famous Hotdogs. She suggested that I go talk with him when there was an opening, but she probably didn't realize that from the moment she told me, I had already began strategizing my approach. I straightened my posture, took a sip of my water, and walked over for my meeting with unknown potential. I was on a mission to see if I could convince the CFO to take some time out of his schedule to come to Molloy and speak with my students. We had a great conversation and I even learned what was really in their hotdogs! Alright, that was a lie, but the rest of the story is real. After a few minutes of speaking, he gave me his business card, which I still have, and told me to reach out to him after the quarter ended. I sent him a follow up "thank you" in the next week and continued to remain in contact with him until I could achieve the goal I set. Surely enough, in the next month, he agreed to come in, and speak to my students. I filled the room with students and even some professors that were interested in taking the opportunity to have a discussion with a CFO.

Throughout the year I brought in many guest speakers, but none of them engaged my students like he did. It is amazing what you can accomplish by simply having the courage to ask for it.

The theme of having the courage to ask for what I wanted continued at the event that Canon attended at the IMA. This event was essential for the next step in my plan because it allowed me to give them my elevator pitch to earn a spot in their summer internship program. Out of a pool of more than 16,000 applicants, only 30 were selected. Out of those 30 people, I filled the last spot of the program. The odds were stacked against me, but through perseverance and poise,

I was chosen over another applicant that had an executive referral. I am strong believer in creating my own luck. My time at Canon greatly impacted me and a part of me holds the hope of returning to work there. Interning at Canon fueled my love of photography. We were given the opportunity to borrow their DSLR cameras for the day and go to the Bronx Zoo to take photos. I ended up breaking away from everyone else and wandering about on my own. I wasn't satisfied with rushing from spot to spot in order to capture the exact same photos as everyone else. I wanted to soak in this rare opportunity and operate at my own pace. When I regrouped with everyone at the end of the day, everyone had wondered where I had gone. So, I showed them. I had captured some excellent photos, most notably a photo of two bears play fighting in a pool of water. Since I had set my camera to take rapid continuous photos I captured the water flying as one bear slapped the other. By the time we returned to the office people that I did not know approached me at my desk to see some of my captures as they heard rumors of what I saw. I fell in love with photography because it taught me the importance of patience and how to enjoy the beauty in the everyday things that surround us. After we returned the camera, I would have to endure a long two years before I would ever hold another DSLR. As much as I wanted to, I could not afford to spend large amount of money on anything, let alone a camera. I felt like a bird with clipped wings. I had so many ideas, but lacked the ability to bring them to life. Aware of my circumstances, I decided to be patient and build towards my opportunity to own one of those beautiful cameras. When I graduated college, I ended up purchasing one as a gift to myself.

The event that I am most proud of from my time as president was "Cupcakes for Cure." The idea came to me in silent reflection and I immediately began strategizing. What I had realized was that there were nearly forty clubs on campus, and although we have the ability to co-host events, we never did. Hosting events individually was not the most effective way to attract campus participation, so I decided that I would break down the walls we had unintentionally put up amongst our clubs. I felt that many of the club leaders did not think of this because our clubs seemed so inherently different. What does the Business and Accounting Club have in common with the Gaming Club, the American Sign Language Club, or even the Anime Club? On the surface, pretty much nothing, but beneath it all we were all people that were passionate about the activities of our club. I figured that the best path to collaboration would be through community service and charity. October was around the corner, so it only made sense to do an event to raise money for breast cancer research. In the first club leaders meeting of the year, I decided to pitch my idea. It went along the lines of this:

"I have been a club president for two years now and I have noticed that as leaders, we tend not to collaborate with other clubs. I feel that it is time that we start thinking outside of the box. Although our clubs may not be connected in nature, we can be connected by a cause. I am asking all of you to consider collaborating with my club in October to raise money for breast cancer research. I am asking that each club that participates donate $25 out of their club budgets in order to start the pool for our donations. Furthermore, I am suggesting that we sell baked goods to students on campus to further supplement the cause. My club will award a prize to the club that raises the most money in the day. Furthermore, for fun, we will acknowledge the club that has the best cupcake design. We may have different passions, but if we stand together for this cause, we can create something meaningful. I know this hasn't been done before, but I think it's time that we start seeing what we have in common, rather than what makes us different. I know that finding a cure to breast cancer is a cause that we can all stand behind."

The idea was well received among the other club leaders and I was presented with the opportunity to coordinate the largest collaboration event that Molloy ever had. I managed to mobilize 25 different clubs and inspire them to join the cause. Not all of the clubs were capable of giving the full $25 that I asked for, but overall, we brought in about $520 before we even sold baked goods.

By the end of the event we had raised about $750. When we were done selling baked goods, I actually walked to each office on campus and asked for donations. My efforts and puppy dog eyes brought in another $75. After this event I became known as the "Charity President" on campus and other club leaders would seek me out to co-host events. It is the responsibility of a leader to inspire others to action and be the guiding force towards their shared vision. I am most proud of this event because I successfully united that which was divided. I saw potential and also had the ability to bring my ideas to life. In the grand scheme of things $800 may not be a lot of money, but to me, it was everything. For the first time in my life, I had convinced people that they had the power to make change on a large scale. These people believed in me and my idea.

Before I could retire, I still had to attend one last Mets game with my club. We raised enough money for my club to pay for all of their tickets and I was proud that I could do that for my students in my last year. There was actually a surprise for all in attendance of the board meeting this year. Unbeknownst to the executive team, Mark Peskin, the CFO of the Mets, dropped in on our meeting. He was hilarious and he brought levity to the room. He then asked us a question, "What do you think the role of the CFO is? And don't tell me the basic answer that he manages the financials." Oddly enough, despite his warning, some of my students did give the obvious answer. On the other hand, I sat with it a minute, and dissected it. When I was sure that I had come to the correct answer, I chimed in, "The role of the CFO is to enhance the value of the company brand." Mark's mouth dropped and he began to pace. After a brief moment of silence he was filled with energy and excitement. He looked at me and said, "I have asked that question for more than twenty years now, and you are the first person to ever answer it correctly." With an enormous smile on my face, I told him, "It took me a second, but I put myself in your shoes and I thought about my job as leader of this club. At the very core of what I do, I try to provide value to my students." He returned my smile and continued to dwell on the fact that I was the first person to ever answer correctly, which made my face sore from smiling even harder. The meeting ended and then I shook the hands of the officers. I was ready to enjoy one last baseball game as club president. When I left the meeting, I checked my phone and as it would turn out on that day I was also awarded a $500 scholarship for my trip to Spain. It was a perfect day. It was the end of my time as the President of the Business and

Accounting Club and the beginning of a new era of exploration and potential. A part of me was sad to let go of the thing that I loved, but when I looked at Nicole and Ryan, my VPs, I knew that I was handing off the torch to the right people. I didn't want them to preserve my legacy, I wanted them to enhance it with their own.

My greatest satisfaction as a leader came in my opportunity to teach. I like to believe that with a single flame that I found within myself, my light illuminated the path for others. Even better, I want to believe that I ignited their path.

Life has been my teacher and it has taught me many difficult lessons. However, throughout everything, I persevered. With tenacity, I held onto the flame that burned inside of me and used all of my will to manifest it into reality. In the palm of my hand, I have all the light that I need to navigate through the darkness. When the winds howled at me, I roared. When the seas swelled, I raged. When confronted by the tempest of fate, I stood in the eye of the storm. I have found the courage within myself to illuminate my own path in the darkness. I will not die like a moth chasing the light of another. I will not chase the flame; I will protect it.

Chapter 14
THE JOURNEY

January 8th, 2018

If you are reading this, know that I have died. Do not mourn me. This is what I wanted.

In the book, Shogun, by James Clavell, I read:

"A man has a false heart in his mouth for the world to see, another in his breast to show to his special friends and his family, and the real one, the true one, the secret one, which is never known to anyone except to himself alone, hidden only God knows where."

I immediately resonated with this quote as I understood the truth behind it. We often hide our true selves from the world and only expose what are willing to lose. I have died twice because I have lost my first two hearts. In the destruction of my youthful innocence, I lost the heart that I shared with my family and friends. In Muga, the death of the ego, I killed the heart that wished to be admired by its peers.

This book is a story from my third heart, my true heart. I am tired of the illusions and lies. I have no interest in maintaining a charade so that I will be accepted by others. I know that revealing my true heart exposes me to great risk. I was afraid of being so honest, but I needed to be; it was the only way that I could show you my conviction.

Life's greatest illusion is death. When we think of the end, we imagine a heart that has stopped beating. However, we are missing the point. Death is the moment when your vision fades to black. Death is all around us; you need only look into the eyes of another person to understand.

My conviction in life has given me the courage to face death. As I stare into the void of black nothingness, I can understand the inevitability of oblivion. The void calls to me singing songs of sweet sleep. However, I am not enchanted by its melody.

I'd much rather compose my own. Although I may have died, I am not dead. The drumming of my heart calls me to wake. With each death of myself, I come closer to the meaning of life.

We are permanence, and impermanence.

We are awake, and we are sleeping.

We are both living and dying.

Make your choice, for every second you are not living, you are just dying. It was in death that I found *the way*.

Still Waters:

I began this project with a fear similar to Willy Loman in *Death of a Salesman*. I was afraid that I was going to die without anything planted in the ground. I was afraid of reaching the end of the road, only to look back and think, *"What if?"* It is the fear of that question that inspires me to take risks and reach for the impossible.

The fact that we are alive and the fact that we are these sentient beings with a profound understanding of the world around us has to mean something. I'm forever perplexed by the simple fact that I am alive and I am capable of thought. I will never fully grasp the fact that I am capable of having an idea and then nurturing it into existence. Can you just take a moment to pause and marvel at how incredible it is that everything around us started as an idea? Imagine you were sent back in time before we had most of the technology of today. Even if you have the knowledge of how, let's say a laptop, works, would you be able to create the first one of that era? Can you even imagine what it was like to have the idea to create the internet? It's fascinating to me how our ideas can grow into everyday realities when we share them with other people.

This life is simply a dream that I need only have the courage to seize control of. I realized that I have everything that I want and you have everything that you want. If you aren't happy with what you have, then start asking yourself to be more and to do more. We are all the summation of what we think we are. We are both the steel of our mind and the hammer that strikes it. The world is not at rigid as we think. The world can bend and morph into something new if we will it to do so. Our choices shape our realities, so start choosing strength. Stop feeding yourself the lie that you are incapable. Stop thinking that you are simply the way you are and cannot change. Life is far too dynamic to hold onto such an arbitrary and debilitating narrative.

The Buddha taught, "Life is suffering." However, the obligation falls upon us to find meaning in our suffering. I find meaning in my tribulations with gratitude. I am grateful for both of my parents. My mother and father both taught me critical lessons throughout life. If I had to choose my parents all over again, I would still choose them. It is the environment that they created, that allowed me to become myself. I believe that my will to fight is innate. However, they provided me with the right situations to use it in. I learned self-reliance, discipline, and tenacity from the world that they created for me. I am grateful for all the feelings that I have felt in life from hatred and fear to love and compassion. Those feelings are a part of who I am and I am not ashamed of any of them. My fears taught me how to have courage and love in my heart. My hatred taught me compassion, empathy, and forgiveness.

We can choose to walk through life with a chip on our shoulder about how unfair the world is and how terrible our circumstances are. Alternatively, we can choose something else. Life is about achieving perspective by learning from the stories of others.

The Alchemist by Paulo Coelho taught me to believe in my personal legend and how to listen to the omens around me. I realized that I was Santiago. I realized that I was the main character of my own story. Likewise, you are the main character of your story. We can live life too afraid to let go of what we have to pursue our destiny or we can choose to run out into uncertainty in hopes of finding the reason why we are alive. His words took ahold of my heart when he explained the feeling that I had, but could never understand:

> *"When you really want something, it is because that desire originated in the soul of the universe. It is your mission earth."*

Man's Search for Meaning by Viktor E. Frankl showed me that even when others try to steal our humanity from us, they cannot dictate how we choose to live. His stories shook me to the core as he explained that even during the Holocaust, the prisoners of Auschwitz could find meaning in life. In the face of genocide, cruelty, and pure evil, some of those innocent people who had everything taken away from them still had the strength to have hope. His stories taught me that, "if you have a 'why' you can figure out any 'how.'"

Good or bad, this life is mine and I am simply grateful to be alive. I bask in the chance to experience the many different facets of the human experience. There is meaning in life and I will spend my days chasing after it. This is my story and I want it to end as a heroic epoch, not a tragedy.

All in:

I have mentioned before that I am not a betting man. However, that is not entirely true. I have been known to clean out my friends in poker when we play Texas Hold'em. They think I am lucky, but the truth is, I just have a better understanding of the game. An undisciplined player can be provoked into betting large amounts when they have junk in their hand. The trick to poker is not in having a good hand, but acting like you do. Many of my friends rely on the "unpredictable approach" where they simply bet big on every turn and eventually get lucky. On the other hand, I only ante up when I am sure that I am going to win and from there it is easy to provoke my friends to feed the pot. I am capable of staying ice cold the entire game and pull off the illusion of being consistent. When I successfully create this atmosphere, the game is mine from that moment on. Although my strategy isn't full proof and I may lose big on a hand, I always win the game. *The funny thing is, even now that they know my strategy, they still won't be able to beat me. I will always have the upper hand because victory is contingent upon execution of a strategy, not knowledge of it.*

There is only one bet that I have ever been willing to make. That bet is on myself. As long as I choose to bet on myself, I will always win. Reflecting on 2017, I can say with confidence that 2017 was the year when I anted up.

I began the year by falling in love with the girl who was named after the stars. In loving her, I learned that I always had the ability to give this love and that I was always worthy of receiving it. I spent most of my life thinking that I was incapable of loving someone as deeply as I love her, but as it would turn out, I just had to wait for the right person to come along.

In late May, I stood tall, and proud. I was the first in my family to graduate college. Getting to college was a dream of mine in high school and I worked tirelessly in order to obtain a substantial academic scholarship. On my own merit, I put myself through college. When times were bleak and money was tight, I always found a way. After my graduation, I was able to fulfill a long term promise I made to myself. I finally bought a DSLR camera that I had wanted more than anything since the first time I picked one up two years ago at Canon. My passion for photography actually aided me tremendously in feeding my creative spirit by immersing myself in nature. Perhaps I can nurture my love for photography into a career, but that is a decision I have to make.

In September, on my birthday, I became involved in two charities. I donated my birthday to Charity Water in order to raise money to help developing nations obtain clean drinking water. Water is something that we take for granted.

While we enjoy our eight glasses a day and our 20-minute showers, each year millions of people die from drinking dirty water that facilitates the contraction of dysentery, typhoid, and diarrheal diseases. The frequency in occurrence for these diseases would substantially decrease if people had access to clean drinking water. I set the ambitious goal of raising ten thousand dollars, but I fell short, only raising $663. At first, I was pretty embarrassed and disappointed that I didn't even come close, but then I realized that I could always try again next year. I may not have achieved my desired goal, but I did raise enough money to give one person 22 months of clean drinking water. On that same day, I signed my paperwork to officially join the Leadership Council of the Family & Children's Association. I had a specific interest in working with youths that have had a difficult upbringing. I want to be able to give them the mentorship and guidance they need in order to help them transition into becoming successful adults after high school. As a member of the council, I also have the responsibility of expanding the reach of the Long Island charity in order to spur a greater degree of community outreach. In our first team meeting, I shared my ideas to make student chapters at colleges and to perhaps host a "TED Talk" at my Alma Mater.

These ideas are currently in motion and I am excited to see what happens. In late October I became the co-host of The Morning Lift Podcast with my one of my best friends, Mike Medina. The podcast was just an idea that sat in our minds for more than a year until we finally got the courage to act on it. We currently have 25 followers on SoundCloud and our most viewed episode has over 100 views, but who knows, maybe one day we will have 25,000 followers and

100,000 views. Regardless of our followership, we believe in our mission. We have the shared goal of inspiring our listeners to better themselves. We deliver our message with sincerity and humor. This has led to some of our followers reaching out to us on social media. Every time we get a message from someone and it says, "That episode was great, it was just what I needed" I smile because it assures me that we are doing something right. One of my friends Andrew thanked me for what I was doing on the podcast. He told me it inspired him to start taking his fitness seriously. Since we started the podcast, he has lost more than 30 pounds and has gotten much stronger. He has even named me his rival and has assured me that he is going to surpass me. Knowing how dedicated he gets, it inspires me to keep working harder to improve myself because he is just as competitive as me. He is not someone who says things unless he means it.

This was also the year that I finally began writing my book. It had been an idea for so long and at times I wasn't sure what to write, but I finally took the leap. Funny enough, it was actually my time at the accounting firm that I used to work for that inspired me to start writing for myself. I was already being published by my accounting firm and in one case, my article was published on the front page of Innovate Long Island. I decided that if I could use my talents for them, I could definitely start using them for myself. In a matter of fact, it was long overdue for me to begin writing for myself. I created a Medium account and started a personal blog. I quickly rose to be ranked as a top writer in the category of inspiration. My articles did not go unnoticed by my friends either and I was incredibly grateful for their support. I actually have to thank my friend Sophia because after reading a few of my articles she said to me, "your articles are amazing, but I don't understand why you just don't write a book." I was caught off guard by the seemingly backhanded compliment. This really got me to reflect on what she said. I had dreamed of writing a book for a long time, but never executed because I wasn't sure if I would have anything of value to say. Honestly, I was just afraid of starting what was a goliath of a task, yet her question sat with me for a while.

Shortly after here inquiry, I stopped writing weekly articles and decided that I would pour all of my energy into writing this book. Getting started proved to be quite difficult while balancing my work schedule and my general need to sleep at some point. I can function pretty efficiently with 4.5-5.5 hours of sleep, but anything less than that and it will be a difficult day. Regardless of how difficult it was, I trudged on through and drank my Death Wish Coffee in the evening to sustain myself. When my time at the accounting firm came to an end in early November, I was left with 17,359 words written. I was proud of what I had accomplished in the past seven months, but I wasn't nearly as close to my goal as I had hoped. I decided to take this time off as a blessing in disguise; I finally had all the time I needed to pour 100% of my attention into creating my best work. In the two months since then I have more than tripled what I started with, and dare I say, completed my first book.

2017 was the year I anted up on my dreams, but 2018 is the year for me to go all in. It is just a coincidence that I would finish my book in the beginning of the new year, but I will still take this as an opportunity for a fresh start. The cards are on the table and it's time to show my hand. I am not afraid of what is to come because I have played my best hand. Although I may lose a great deal, I will never lose everything.

The End:

As I commit these last thoughts to paper, the feeling is surreal. I cannot help but thank you, my reader, for being a part of my journey and allowing me to be a part of yours. We all have questions that burn inside of us that demand answering and I think I have come to understand mine.

What is my purpose?
Why does this inspire me?
How will I create my legacy?

I understand that I was born with purpose and as long as I choose to live with intention, I will achieve it. I want to dedicate my life to helping other people throughout the world because I am inspired by the ingenuity and resilience of humanity when faced with an obstacle. Creativity is the key to solving the most pressing issues of our generation and I know that I can contribute to that effort. I will create my legacy by committing myself to the mission of "creating a kinder world."

Allow me to look at the night sky just one more time before I finish talking. It has been a while since I truly took in the wonder of the heaven above me. I can't believe how much time has passed since when I last looked at you. Yet, you still look just as mesmerizing. It has always been so easy for me to get lost in your beauty. Even as a child I found myself bewitched by the allure of your shades of blue midnight. You were the first to give me perspective about my existence. You taught me the most important lesson: the sky above is not just one thing, but a collection of similar parts bound together. "Although we are small when we stand alone, we are not powerless. Together we are as infinite as the sky overhead."

One day I will read this book and think one of two things. Either, "This is where it all began" or I will ask myself, "What happened to that kid?" I am not ready to let go of this dream, so please just allow me to have it just a little longer. Do not be sad that this is the end, this just a new beginning.

So now you must ask yourself, *"Where will I go now?"*

If you seek your answers, the omens will speak to you. Be sure to the listen when they speak because sometimes their voices are carried on a whisper, a gentle breeze, or the pale light of the yellow moon. Just remember one thing:

You are free . . .

Epilogue

May 8th, 2023

Ah freedom, young Ethan, do you even know what it means to be free, yet you want it so badly?

I've realized that true peace is achieved by fixing our relationship with time. Many of us do not live synchronized lives with the time we experience. For example, those of us troubled by events of the past live in the past, and those who struggle with anxiety, try to live in the future. The truth is, our only peace is in the present moment. There is no guarantee of tomorrow, and the sooner you realize that the sooner you can begin living your life.

I've also realized that events are not emotional, people are. That being said, am I saying to ignore all your emotions? No, I am saying that we have the ability to regulate how we feel. external circumstances can influence our internal worlds, but ultimately, your will is the arbiter of reason. You can rationalize surrender and victimhood, or you can rationalize a solution to your problems. Sometimes, bad things just happen, and we have to deal with the consequences. However, even the worst moments of our lives can lead to the best, and our best to the worst.

Often times it is those that we love the most that end up hurting us. Even years after separating from these people whether it be parents, friends, or significant others, the pain they gave us is there, despite them not being around to inflict more. We carry the pain, we carry the wounds and oftentimes come to identify with that experience since it had such a profound effect on our lives. Even when we think we have overcome it, I think more often than not, the first round of "overcoming it" is suppression. We internalize the pain and learn to flex our muscles differently to avoid sharp shooting pains. We accept that our needs will never be met and that it is better to simply roll with the punches.

The problem with this coping mechanism, in my experience, is that doesn't fix the root pain. You simply learn to brush it off so it doesn't hurt you, or use it as fuel to the fire. You hide the pain or have adjusted enough to get by in regular society without being a loon, but when someone tries to get closer to you they have to dig through wall after wall of emotional shielding. The wall will not be overlooked by your partner too, they will want to dig deeper, and you will have no choice but to lower your guard. You'll try to trust and be open, and if all goes well, you two are closer for doing it, or it opens you up for a direct strike to the heart.

Are you stuck in the past, trying to live in the present moment? Are past events influencing your emotions of today? It can sneakily get in the way of building deeper relationships with those around you.

As for my friends determined to live in the future, more often than not, money has us living in the future. We burn our spirit on high trying to ascend faster and faster to catch up with the money floating in the ether, yet, there is always that fear. If you don't have a lot of money, odds are you are in a constant state of fear. You fear not having enough, and when the utility bills come in you're afraid to check the price. When you need to open the bank app on your phone, you dread seeing your balance. There is so much pain about the future, and most of it comes from money.

We think our lives are not beautiful right now, and that they will only be exactly what we want in the future. There is truth that the future can be better; however, before tomorrow, comes today. You need to start finding a way to be comfortable in the present moment. Think about your life outside of all the fear and stimulation. Think outside of your job, your appointments, the kids' baseball game, or anything else.

Sit down with yourself honestly, and ask yourself, "Who am I outside of all these personas, outside of this ego I project to the world?"

What do you look like underneath your mask of civility? Are you just playing a role or are you living life on your terms? Are you happy? Are you free?

It's okay if you have never thought to ask yourself this, and it is okay if it makes you feel a variety of emotions from sad, angry, bitter, unsure, or "this guy is so annoying."

To those who burn themselves out trying to force themselves into the future, I challenge you to get up early and catch one sunrise, if you can, go to the beach, and just integrate yourself into that moment. Detach from all of the fear, the stress, and the masks, just be you. Sit in the silence, and breathe deeply. Open your eyes, and see that life, is beautiful, you just need to slow down a little. We are all going to die one day, so don't be in such a rush for tomorrow, seize the day.

I imagine time as integers from -1 to +1, the negative is the past, the positive is the future, and 0 is the present moment. Everyone falls somewhere on that spectrum in terms of where the majority of their emotions come from.

Now imagine that in between the scale of -1 +1, there is a moving slider of 1, like the notch on a ziplock bag. Imagine the goal is to get as close to zero as possible, if your scale is all the way to the left it sums to a negative one (-1+ 0). If it is all the way to the right, it sums to a positive one (0+1). Thus making your emotional outlook slightly skewed to either direction while searching for the present moment, 0.

It's a simple test, now apply it to yourself, and come to an understanding if you are living your life primarily based on past or present decisions. If you are negatively skewed, that means past trials and tribulations shape your reality of today. You can also have past events that inspire you; however, even in that case, it is not ideal to linger on accomplishments of the past. You should have time to appreciate your past accomplishments, but you cannot make your entire identity about the moment you peaked. If you are positively skewed, that is a little better because you are looking towards new outcomes, rather than reliving old ones. It is good that you look to the future, and are hopeful for the possibility of change. However, your obsession of the future will rob you of your youth, peace, and ability to be in the present moment. Sometimes work can wait, you need to take a mental health day, or you should realize that by changing today, you can create a better tomorrow.

Ultimately, I think we should try our best to score -0.5 + 0.5 = 0. We can take a healthy appreciation of our past, learn from past moments, or feel the joy of past success to inspire us to create more moments of success. We can also look to the future with optimism, for good things to come, rather than, in a constant state of panic and fear.

In the zero, we find our connection to the present moment, a balanced life, and appreciation for the simple pleasures around us. Imagine today was your last day, and there was nothing you could do about it, factually, all that you know, or could learn is not enough to save you. Today is the day you die, in the moments before death takes you, will you feel sad? Will you regret not putting more on the table, or will you be happy with the way you lived, proud of it even?

Just because we don't have to think about death on a daily basis, does not mean he is not there, looming overhead counting the grains of sand in your hourglass. If you are negative, you will cling to the grain of sand as it falls, helpless to fight against gravity, if you are positively charged you will try to make the sand fall faster. Despite how many pieces of sand you cling to, they will still follow the flow of gravity, and for all you want the sand to fall faster, there will come a point when you are begging it to slow down.

Life has felt so odd to me these last few years in between. There has been so much turmoil in our country, there has been sickness, conspiracy, division, and racial tensions, or at least, that's what the world wants you to think. I think that the real battle is that it is just getting harder and harder to live. Rent is too high, food is more expensive, and the 40-hour workweek is an antiquated term of the past. It can feel like that no matter how hard we work, there is just never enough, we are fed just enough not to bite the hand that feeds, but never enough to really nourish ourselves, and enrich our lives. The minimum wage went up but look at the price of everything else. We could make $15 an hour, but that doesn't mean much considering rents in NY are about $2500 a month for a one-bedroom.

In the years after writing "The Ink of My Soul and The Fire In My Bones," there were many highs and lows. I had times when I moved out of New York, to New Jersey and Florida. I married that special lady that wrote about in the previous chapters, but we also divorced. My dog cheated death with surgery for a time, but then the reaper came. I had months when I made $15,000 in a month and I thought everything was finally going to be okay, and then there were times when I lost $20,000. I went from living with family to my first home with my wife, to our dream home, and then to being displaced in the world.

Despite the many ups and downs of my life, I don't look at my past self in a negative light. I don't regret any of the words I wrote, and I hope the honest depiction of my experiences may have helped you feel a little more understood, or helped you understand yourself better. I think we are all starved for connection, especially after COVID-19 when we locked ourselves away for 2 years.

You aren't broken, a failure, or "never going to make it." You are just you, and it is time to just sit down with that fact even your name is a lie.

Your name isn't you! Crazy thought right?

Your name is just a word that is used to try and describe you. Some people have some amazing names that their parents agonized over before deciding on the name they gave you, and others are named nanes that are . . . not quite as inspiring. My point is, that your name is just a name, it is not you.

All your emotional pain, and triumph, are based on an idea that you have of you, if you are unhappy with where you are in life, the only thing that separates you from your goal is time and effort. Break down the mindset of what makes your current self, then challenge it, reconstruct it, and let it work for you. We were once formless but then adopted form. Although having order is important, you have to be careful to not starve yourself of your humanity.

Looking back on my thoughts from this book, I see the ways that I have grown, some opinions of mine have changed, and some unexpected things happened along the way. I still think that piece of me is still alive and kicking inside of me, like a *horcrux*. I still have a desire to succeed, and to see how much more I have on the table. I'm honestly even more fired up than ever before.

From my heart to yours, don't let bitterness seep into yours. Don't view the world as hopeless, and your dreams as romantic. Go to the place you buried your dreams and dig them up again. It is never too late to try again, you aren't too old, or too broken. As long as there is life in those lunges, and a fire in your bones, you can choose to keep fighting.

In my reflection, I realized that I was one of those people so focused on the future, that I sacrificed all of the present moment. I was forever in a rush for the future, hoping for better days, but missed that "today" is always better than yesterday or tomorrow.

When I have my coffee in the morning, I always take a moment to indulge in that first sip. When I hold my dog Tsuki, I *hold* her and play with her. When I speak with my family, they have my full attention.

When I find myself fearing the future, or lingering in the past, I just try to close my eyes, find my center, and bring myself back into the present moment. You are consciousness piloting a time machine and experiencing time; however, the machine only goes in one direction. We are just a toy wound up that will eventually run out of steps. Do not cling to the pain or glory of the past, and do not fear or fret for the future, instead, go with time. Surrender to the flow of time and accept that as long as you live your life with intention today, everything else will work itself out. Don't get paralyzed by the problem, search for the solution, and find the strength within yourself to become all that you dream of.

Lastly, thank you to you, my reader. Thank you for reading my book, and I hope that some of my experiences resonated with you. At the end of the day, we are all human, I typed this story with the ink of my soul and wrote it in the universal language, love.

I encourage you to live well, stop to smell the roses every once in a while and keep fighting for your dreams no matter how old you are. Your life is just a seed in the earth, and the world grows where you put your intention. Don't let life pass you, when you breathe, feel it with all of your body. When you take a bite of good food savor it! When you are with someone you love, love them as deeply as you can. Our lives are just little flickers of light in the darkness, yet, they carry so much weight to them. We are fleeting, temporary things, but it is our impermanence that makes our experience beautiful.

Do not be afraid, you have the solution to every problem you face. Trust yourself to find them.

Special Thanks

First, I would like to thank Justin Scharff for acting as the editor of my book. Thank you for providing me with invaluable feedback throughout the course of writing this book. You have been my best friend since I was five and I have always been able to rely on you.

Second, Asvini Serasundera. You are the love of my life and my creative muse. You have always pushed me to strive for the impossible.

Lastly, Sophia Ouloupis. You said the words that pushed me over the edge and helped me realize that the time to write this book had come.

About the Author

NASM-CPT
NCBTMB
NYS Realtor
B.S. Accounting

Ethan is a soul on fire, that wants to share his spark with others.

"I grew up humbly. I lived with my brother and two brothers growing up. We also had a miniature schnauzer named Fritz. We figured the name was appropriate since he was a German dog.

"Growing up, I had this big chip on my shoulder. I felt I never really got my fair chance to succeed, but I was determined to create it for myself. Many kids rebelled when young, but my rebellion was personal excellence. I never quite felt that I was good enough, or worse, I felt I was caught in the purgatory of better than normal but still not excellent.

"I was told I was a failure, and that I was fat and stupid so many times that it drove me to prove others wrong. I wanted to prove to them, and to myself, that I was none of those things. This led me to go internal at times, completely locking down my emotions and feelings of self-doubt to allow myself to push past whatever barrier was in my way.

"I felt like I crawled to my feet and out of the dirt. Every day it felt like I was able to crawl an inch when everyone around me was going a mile. I was jealous of the opportunities that fell into the laps of others when I felt so starved. I realized that the only way to crawl out of the dirt was to become undeniable, becoming a diamond in the rough. I had an intense internal pressure to succeed so that I didn't get left behind in the life that I wanted. This was the source of all my drive, this unwavering desire to just be free, and escape the circumstances of my environment. I just wanted a slice of peace in my life, so that I could finally just take a breath.

"Over the years, I realized that this anger inside of me was chewing me up. I never let my anger spill out onto others, but I was never kind to myself either. I struggled to see the value in myself or my accomplishments. I started to turn my lens inward with meditation and writing to help sift through my thoughts. I needed to face these emotions inside of me, to understand them, and let them go. It's always going to be a work in progress; however, through introspection, we can clear the blockage from our mind to our heart. We can learn to lower our guard but still maintain self-worth.

"There are so many times I have felt defeated and beaten down by life, but the number one thing I have learned is that 'There is *always a way.' The way may be through hellfire, but so be it; you have to be prepared to endure it all to make it through to the other side. Through patience, meditation, and an unrelenting work ethic, I carved out the piece of myself that could make it out of my personal hell."*

www.ingramcontent.com/pod-product-compliance
Lightning Source LLC
Chambersburg PA
CBHW071933160426
43198CB00011B/1378